PRAISE FOR
ATTACHED TO GOD

What a refreshing and uncynical confrontation of the toxic spirituality that many of us inherited from our intimate relationships. This book looks at how God transcends the brokenness to meet us where we are. Krispin has written a practical resource that intersects both character work and spiritual formation for many of us who are trying to find the God that is better and more reliable than even our most intimate relationships.

BRANDI MILLER, host of *Reclaiming My Theology*

This book normalizes our insecurities about God and faith. It gives us language for understanding our patterns of seeking closeness, untangles us from bad theology concerning mental health, and invites us on a realistic journey to wholeness. Full of psychological research and theological insight, this book is a gift.

PEACE AMADI, PsyD, professor and
author of *Why Do I Feel Like This?*

If you have found your faith squeezed into various boxes of shame, anxiety, and disillusionment, *Attached to God* is a shaft of light. This book is like therapy and theology: it will gently bloom you open and graciously begin the work of repair. Krispin's wisdom is field-tested and filled with story, evidence, and Scripture. Krispin brings us back to the places where harm set in, exposing that the fault was not with us but with the fault lines of the structures we were handed, then by degrees walks us toward a solid and secure foundation. Thank you, Krispin, for being our guide through this terrain.

J. S. PARK, interfaith hospital chaplain
and author of *The Voices We Carry*

This is a powerful book for anyone struggling to relate deeply and openly with God. Reading it touched me in profound ways and has helped me heal from the distorted messages I've received about how God wants to connect with me!

SHARON HALE, LMFT, president of the Portland Center for Emotionally Focused Therapy

Attached to God makes me so happy and hopeful! This is such important information for people trying to make sense of their relationship with God. Many of us struggle with a faith life that leaves us feeling anxious or disconnected in different ways no matter what we do. In relatable and easy-to-grasp language, Krispin reveals how this happens through the science of human attachment. In doing so, he offers us hope to step out of the pull of our messy, imperfect attachment histories and into a more secure relationship with God.

JEFFREY OLRICK, PhD, cofounder of Growing Connected and author of *The 6 Needs of Every Child*

A brilliant blend of attachment science and spiritual development, *Attached to God* will help you understand more about yourself, about the people around you, and about God. Mayfield deftly challenges Christian teachings based in shame, guilt, and "should," pointing instead to the individual and unique ways that each of us can connect with a loving and graceful God.

ROBERT VORE, therapist and cohost of *CXMH: A Podcast on Faith & Mental Health*

Growing up in church was confusing and hard because when I struggled in life, I thought it was because I didn't pray hard enough. In this book, Krispin articulated everything I have grown to understand but never really had the words to express. This book will give you better understanding and help you create a deeper relationship with God.

CELESTE VICIERE, host of *Celeste the Therapist* podcast

ATTACHED TO GOD

ATTACHED TO GOD

A PRACTICAL GUIDE TO DEEPER
SPIRITUAL EXPERIENCE

KRISPIN MAYFIELD

ZONDERVAN BOOKS

ZONDERVAN BOOKS

Attached to God
Copyright © 2022 by Krispin Mayfield

Requests for information should be addressed to:
Zondervan, *3900 Sparks Dr. SE, Grand Rapids, Michigan 49546*

Zondervan titles may be purchased in bulk for educational, business, fundraising, or sales promotional use. For information, please email SpecialMarkets@Zondervan.com.

ISBN 978-0-310-36382-8 (audio)

Library of Congress Cataloging-in-Publication Data

Names: Mayfield, Krispin, 1986- author.
Title: Attached to God : a practical guide to deeper spiritual experience / Krispin Mayfield, LPC.
Description: Grand Rapids : Zondervan, 2022. | Includes bibliographical references. | Summary: "If you've ever heard the damaging message that feeling far from God is your own choice or the result of sin in your life, therapist Krispin Mayfield's Attached to God will reveal a new way of approaching your relationship with the Divine that will help you feel closer and more connected to God than ever before"—Provided by publisher.
Identifiers: LCCN 2021037016 (print) | LCCN 2021037017 (ebook) | ISBN 9780310363798 (trade paperback) | ISBN 9780310363804 (ebook)
Subjects: LCSH: Hidden God. | God—Knowableness. | Spiritual life—Christianity.
Classification: LCC BT180.H54 M28 2022 (print) | LCC BT180.H54 (ebook) | DDC 231.7—dc23/eng/20211201
LC record available at https://lccn.loc.gov/2021037016
LC ebook record available at https://lccn.loc.gov/2021037017

Cover design: Lindy Martin / Faceout Studio
Cover images: Maria Mirnaya / Grisha Bruev / Shutterstock
Interior design: Kait Lamphere

Printed in the United States of America

22 23 24 25 26 27 28 29 30 /LSC/ 14 13 12 11 10 9 8 7 6 5 4 3 2 1

For Ransom and Ramona,
who have helped me deeply understand
how God feels toward me
and have brought absolute joy and delight to my life

CONTENTS

FOREWORD

When I was about four years old, I learned in Sunday school that my life was like a black-and-white picture. A deep gorge of sin separated me from God, but Jesus's death on the cross built a bridge across. My kind but stern teacher wagged her finger at our class and said that the only way not to be separated from God and fall into the chasm of death was to step onto the bridge to make it to the other side.

Being something of a teacher's pet and decidedly against dying, I decided if God was on the other side of that bridge, I better commit to getting across it. I spent my whole childhood walking across that bridge, trying to make the God on the other side smile at how diligent I was.

As my friend Krispin Mayfield describes in this book, I had a shame-based attachment style with God. Striving for perfection was how I felt seen by the God on the other side of the bridge, and feeling shutdown was how I prodded myself to keep running toward him.

In college, my theology professor's wife invited me to be a part of a weekly small group in their home with a motley crew of other overly ambitious women. For the first time in my life, I experienced a person in a role of authority showing me a spirituality where I was allowed to slow down. One cold December day before Christmas break, Tabitha handed me a copy of *Dakota* by Kathleen Norris. I snatched it with a smile, excited to read it because, frankly, being the teacher's pet that I am, I would have read anything she said I should.

I read *Dakota* in the back seat of my family's packed suburban as we drove across the frozen tundra of South Dakota on our way to Montana for vacation. "Maybe seeing the Plains is like seeing an icon," Norris says. "What seems stern and almost empty is merely open, a door into a simple and holy state."[1]

On the I-90 bridge over the Missouri River, I remember looking out through my half-iced-over window at the crystalline blue sky and snowy ground on the other side of the river and feeling a deep, whole-body peace. Maybe I didn't have to cross bridges to get to God.

I met Krispin Mayfield on social media over, I believe, a Twitter thread about integrating psychology and theology. At that time in my career as a new author, I ached for a friend and colleague who would treat me like a collaborator rather than competition. Let's just say I had experienced too much of the latter and far too little of the former to believe I could walk into my vocation with safety and confidence. Krispin sought me out and struck up a friendship, and over many hours' worth of Voxer and WhatsApp messages, his kindness gave me space not only to feel more seen as an author in our field but also to feel safe and strong. He is a friend who is never judgmental or inconvenienced by your struggles but, rather, has an uncanny ability to show you that you are worthy of love.

The same presence Krispin has offered me as a friend and

colleague is what you will find within the pages of *Attached to God*. In the chapters ahead, I pray you will dare to stand beside Krispin to look at the Plains of your perceived distance from God. Let his insights about your attachment style be like an icon. What appears flat or even frustrating is merely open space—a window into the world of your already-loved and precious soul. Let the practices he has offered in these chapters be an invitation to stop running and striving and to let all that has been shut down and silenced be soothed by kindness.

May the wilderness of your wounds and weariness become the place where you hear that you are already and always held.

K.J. Ramsey, licensed professional counselor and author of *This Too Shall Last*

INTRODUCTION

I suppose this book started when I was fifteen years old, on a beach in Thailand.

Two and a half years earlier, when I was twelve, my parents moved our family from Southern Oregon to a huge metropolis in central China. We left the small town where I'd been born and raised, crossing the globe to be missionaries. Every single thing about life was different, including church.

I'd grown up in a white nondenominational church, mostly middle class, with few demographic exceptions. Most of my Christian upbringing came from the evangelical organization Focus on the Family, a limited circle of Christian publishers, and Saturday night TBN, where I religiously watched *Carman: Video Gold*, a show featuring a solid thirty minutes of Carman's music videos every single week. Most Christians I knew had a similar background of faith and learned from the same Christian leaders I did. Then suddenly, in one overseas move, my religious world instantly expanded.

In China our church was composed of a community of missionaries from across the world and from a variety of church backgrounds. We met in living rooms, sharing responsibilities of leading worship songs and teaching from the Bible, followed by a lunch together at a local restaurant. In this diverse spiritual community, I learned that relationship with God was more than just memorizing Bible verses, telling people about Jesus, and doing the right things. I learned about passionate worship, charismatic prayer, reading the Bible for myself, and hearing God speak directly to me through the Holy Spirit. It was in that small house church that I first felt real closeness with God, as well as real feelings of distance.

At the beginning of my freshman year, the month I turned fifteen, I experienced a visceral sense of God's presence for the first time. When a new missionary arrived, he showed me a more intimate kind of worship where I pleaded with God to be close to me. In response, I could feel the spirit of God with me, moving me to tears. It was unlike any experience I'd had before, like my black-and-white faith came into full living color.

But in less than two months, I noticed that God was inconsistent in answering my call for closeness. One Sunday I felt overwhelming peace; the next I felt nothing. The hardest part, though, was the bewildering confusion: I'd stumbled across something wonderful, but I couldn't figure out why the connection was so unstable. I didn't know what brought God close and what interfered. Long before I'd even heard the term *attachment science*, I was trying to figure out the science of connection with God, trying to identify what wasn't working and why.

That year, our family left the cold winter to spend two weeks in Thailand, the go-to vacation destination of many missionaries in China. I wanted to stay local, despite the freezing weather, to hang out with my friends and practice with my band, Sanctified

Viscosity (we thought *viscosity* meant viciousness; only later did we find out it was a scientific term for the density of a liquid). But of course my parents forced me to go with them on a two-week vacation to the tropical beaches of Phuket. It was *so* annoying.

I spent each evening alone, watching the sunset on the beach, the sand slowly cooling beneath me as I scribbled away in a journal. I fitfully tried to figure out the mechanics of closeness with God, sketching out diagrams and flowcharts replete with arrows and boxes. I was trying to create a map that would help me connect the dots. My sketches tried to arrange concepts like confession, prayer, worship, silence, close, far, and periods of testing in a way that would help me figure out how to get close. In the end, it seemed that feeling close to God correlated with my behavior, but the pattern wasn't consistent enough to say for sure.

The most frustrating part was that I'd greatly expanded my repertoire of ways to connect with God. My range was much larger than the basics I'd learned in elementary Sunday school. So what was it going to take to feel as though God was near? I wanted to live in the overwhelming peace I felt on those first Sunday mornings. Instead, it felt like an on-again, off-again romantic relationship, making my spiritual life a tumultuous storm, not at all like the fountain of peace I'd been promised. After a while I couldn't help but wonder how God *really* felt about me.

Amid the turbulence of adolescence, instead of providing needed stability, my relationship with God became a source of heartache and shame. I presumed something was wrong with me and my best bet was to try to be a better me, someone more worthy of God's nearness. So I set out on a journey for closeness, down a path of Bible college and ministry, and I will tell you the end before I tell you the middle—none of it worked. Fifteen years after sketching my diagrams on the beach, I still couldn't close the gap between me and God with any consistency.

It wasn't until I'd been a practicing therapist for some years that I noticed there are patterns for how we reach out for connection—not unlike the diagrams in my notebook at age fifteen. As I walked with people through their relational universes, I saw how we all find ourselves starving for connection at one time or another. And when we feel that starvation, we have different ways of trying to get the connection we long for.

In time, I researched what is known as *attachment science*. Formerly known as attachment theory, attachment science is the science of relationships and, specifically, what we do when we feel the need for connection.

When I'm working with couples or individuals, I have one focus when they come into my office: I want to help them examine the ways they reach out for closeness. We look carefully at these behaviors, investigating whether each one helps or makes the distance feel worse. We also look at how these behaviors affect those around them. As we investigate the map they've been given—the patterns they were taught for seeking closeness—we find better ways to feel the closeness they long for.

In this book we're going to do the same, only in relationship with God. We're going to look at the ways you've been taught to seek closeness with God, why they either work out or wear you out, and how your specific needs can point you down a healthier path. To start sorting between the healthy and unhealthy, we need a basic framework for healthy ways of getting close and what methods only make the distance feel worse. Fortunately, attachment science has been studying the behaviors we use to get the closeness we need for over half a century.

Of course, reaching out to an invisible God is different from reaching out to others in our lives. Philip Yancey asks, "How do you sustain a relationship with a being so different from any other, imperceptible by the five senses?"[1] So much of relationship happens in the nonverbals. It's someone's face lighting up when their eyes meet ours. It's scooting a little closer on the couch or giving a hug that says we care. It's in the body language and the feelings our tones convey, the background music of the actual words between us. So a relationship with God can often be perplexing and sometimes maddening.

But we don't have to stay in that state of confusion. There are clearly defined categories for reaching out to others that also apply to reaching out to God. They are like maps we can use for finding our Creator. These categories give us a helpful framework to understand how we relate to God, how this illuminates our own areas of insecurity, and what we need to feel more secure. This is the power of attachment science. It helps us understand why we reach for closeness in the ways that we do, as well as why those ways work—or don't.

HEAD VERSUS HEART

Attachment science tells us how we *feel* in relationships. Do we feel safe and secure? Do we feel tentative or anxious? In the church, we know what we *think* about our relationship with God, but that can be different from how we *feel* about it. Cognitively, we know God is like the father in Jesus's prodigal son story, but sometimes we experience God more like a tyrant than a loving parent. We've been told that because of Jesus's work, we're at peace with God, yet we feel the constant hint of disapproval. We might say we know God loves us unconditionally, but we worry that the moment we slip up, God will pull away.

It's hard to put words to these feelings, often because we think we're not supposed to have them. A few years ago, a study was conducted where Christians were asked to consider a way of describing God—attributes like kind, patient, responsive—and to identify whether the adjectives were ones they felt they "should believe that God is like" or that they "personally feel that God is like."[2] At the end of the study, the researchers found that although people did experience God as a positive figure in their lives, participants said that their experience of God was not as positive as they believed it *should be*. This confirms what many of us already know: in most church communities, we're afraid to talk about our insecurities with God because we feel we should not have them.

The vulnerable space of acknowledging these discrepancies is a sacred one. It's a wonderful privilege to walk into these waters with people as they tell me things like, "I've always been told that 'Jesus loves me, this I know, for the Bible tells me so,' but deep down, I feel like God doesn't really want me and isn't going to stick around. I've never really put that into words. It's just been this background feeling my whole life." When we can slow down and notice how we feel about God, it helps us understand our attachment style and how it affects our relationship with God.

I hope that as you read this book, you notice not only what

your head knows but also what your gut feels. As we walk through these common ways of relating to God, notice how you reach for closeness in other relationships in your life, and take some time considering if this type of attempt at closeness also shows up in your relationship with God.

Chapter One

THE STILL FACE
OF GOD

If you are confused about how relationship with God works, you are not alone. In the church, we're told that closeness is a black-and-white experience. As Billy Graham said, "When we truly believe in Jesus and sincerely commit our lives to Him—then our lives will be changed!"[1] Once we set foot into faith, God is no longer a faraway unknown; God is close to us. But in our actual experience, relationship with God can be much more confusing. We do not feel as close to God as we've been told we should or would. We want closeness, and we strive to make it happen. Then even when we know we're close, something still feels amiss, like we're not wanted.

Of course, there are other times when we feel we're wrapped in God's embrace, so close that we could reach out and touch our Divine Parent. Whether it's a mystical experience in a charismatic church service, or a calm, grounded sense of God's love in the middle of a forest, or a moment in community that gives us a deep sense of belonging, most of us have experienced moments when the invisible God becomes tangible in some way. But we don't often live there.

Why does God's presence sometimes feel closer than our breath but at other times God's face seems hidden from us? We can feel held like a child at some points of our faith journey and utterly abandoned at others—as if God is playing hide-and-seek and we're desperately trying to figure out where and when and why he hides. We try to read the map we've been given but find ourselves wandering through the wilderness.

Then this confusing experience is made worse by the formulas we're given by our faith communities. In his book *The Purpose Driven Life*, Rick Warren tells us, "You're as close to God as you choose to be."[2] This becomes salt in the wound when we desperately want God to be close but experience only absence. If we feel far from God, we assume it's because we're not taking the steps, not because we don't have an accurate map. If we don't feel close, it must be our unwillingness to take the trek that keeps us apart.

After all, when it comes to distance, God can't be the problem. So in a two-factor scenario like a personal relationship with God, distance leads to the inevitable conclusion: the problem is me. I must be selfish, lazy, or self-absorbed. So to prove we are none of those things, we continue to trudge along the path we've been pointed down. Along the way, we add item after item to the to-do list: Get up early for devotions. Volunteer for a ministry we don't have time for. Search our lives for overlooked sin. Join a small group and commit time to it (even if it's unhealthy or unhelpful). We try not to buckle under the weight of these requirements because they seem to be essential to getting close to God. If we are far from God, we figure it's because of our own shortcomings.

But the reality is that distance happens in all relationships. Couples fight. Good friends can go weeks without a text message. Parents simply can't be with their kids 24/7. A relationship with God is no different. God sometimes feels close and sometimes feels farther than the moon.

Rather than only one map to guide us close to God, we've been given a whole stack. Christian books, sermons, denominational traditions, family members—each has a slightly different take on what it means to grow in closeness with God. These maps give us an overwhelming amount of information. But sometimes that information seems to conflict. Over time, we find that some maps point us in the right direction, and others seem promising but leave us wandering in circles, exhausted and confused.

FEELING INSECURE

Ours was a *Sesame Street* family, but on occasion I would catch episodes of *Mister Rogers' Neighborhood* on PBS. I still remember how Mr. Rogers would turn to the camera and say, "I like you just the way you are." It speaks to the need we have not only as children but as humans. It's balm for the soul, a statement that creates safety and security. Being liked for who we are is an invitation into calm in the presence of another. It's true closeness.

The affirmations that Mr. Rogers regularly spoke directly to the camera reflected his life's work. After ordination in

1963, he dedicated his ministry to making sure American children everywhere knew they were loved, using a relatively new technology: television. Now an icon, informally known by many as Saint Fred, he has become the picture of relentless empathy and kindness—essentially being love with a sweater on. *Mister Rogers' Neighborhood* was a small yet meaningful grace for children who didn't have an adult in their lives who could communicate the love they needed. He knew that each person needs to know they are loved just the way they are.

Yet it seems Mr. Rogers had trouble believing that God loved him just as *he* was. At age seventy-four, he was at home, dying of stomach cancer and about to slip into a coma that he wouldn't wake up from. His wife of fifty years was at his side when he asked a heartbreaking question: "Am I a sheep?"[3]

He was referring to Matthew 25, in which Jesus speaks of the coming judgment where the Son of Man will separate the sheep from the goats on the basis of whether they cared for the marginalized. In this teaching, the Son of Man says to the unfortunate goats, "Depart from me" (v. 41). This separation is our greatest fear when we desperately want to be close.

In Mr. Rogers's question, we see a poignant glimpse of his insecurity. He wondered whether he was good enough or whether he would be judged and separated from God forever. It's easy for me to imagine him leaving this life to be embraced by the God he loved and served for decades. Yet Mr. Rogers himself couldn't trust that he was lovable enough to be accepted. Turns out even the most saintly of us feel insecure with God sometimes. And it's what we do in these times of insecurity that makes all the difference.

Attachment Science

Attachment science is the study of how we get and keep connection with others. How we attach affects relationships, mental health, and development. The field started when psychologist Dr. John Bowlby demonstrated in the 1950s that children need an emotional connection with a caregiver and has since expanded to examine how people of all ages need connection with others.

As I walk with people through their relational universes, I can see how we all find ourselves starving for connection at one time or another. And when we feel that starvation, we have different ways of trying to get the connection we long for.

Attachment science is the study of the ways we get and keep connection with others. Psychology professors often introduce this field to their students by showing a well-known video of an experiment called the still face experiment. A one-year-old sits in a high chair, and the mom faces her, smiling and playing. Then the mother lets her face go blank. She's not interactive or responsive; she has a "still face." The baby begins cooing, trying to get her mother's attention. Then she points around the room, trying to see if at least her mom's eyes will move to where she's pointing. Then she begins to cry, and within minutes she is melting down. The experiment shows her need for connection and when it disappears, all the behaviors she employs to get it back. Cooing, pointing, crying—all these gestures are designed to bring her mother close again. It's her one-year-old map for regaining connection.

We are built for closeness, and when those we love go "still face," we can hardly bear it. We *feel* the distance, even if they're right in the room with us. And we have to regain connection somehow. Disconnection demands a response.

Sometimes we experience the still face of God. Of course, God is close—God is omnipresent—but we don't *feel* close. We're not getting any signals. Christian tradition has often called this "the dark night of the soul." Saints great and small have reported walking through these times, part of the mountain-and-valley life of faith.

Mother Teresa, who spent her whole life ministering in the slums of Calcutta, experienced the still face of God for years. In a letter to her spiritual director, she exposed the harrowing distance she felt: "When the pain of longing is so great—I just long & long for God—and then it is that I feel—He does not want me—He is not there."[4] As with the baby in the experiment, she finds that all her maps for reconnection don't work, writing, "Sometimes—I just hear my own heart cry out—'My God' and nothing else comes." As she lived for decades without the closeness she longed for, she lost composure, living with a "torture and pain I can't explain."[5] While not everyone feels this pain for decades, most of us experience the still face of God at one time or another.

I see the still-face scenario play out with couples all the time. A small conflict arises, sometimes just a change in tone of voice or shift in body language, and a rift opens between them. They both feel the disconnection, just like the baby and her mother in the still face experiment. In that moment, a dark cloud comes over the room as they sense the distance between them. And then, nearly instantaneously, they respond. They don't point or coo or cry, but they have their own ways of trying to regain closeness. Let me tell you, some methods work better than others.

Stop for a minute and think about how you respond when you feel a rift between you and someone you care about. Do you storm the castle to sort it out, frantically trying to close the distance? Or maybe you stuff your feelings down in the basement of your heart, ignoring the pain, patiently waiting for the smoke to clear before you can be close again. Or maybe you beat yourself up for causing the rupture in the first place, wondering if you're even built for relationships.

There are a variety of paths we take in the journey for closeness, and while some of them get us there, some don't. These differences point to types of *attachment styles*. And we don't use them only with parents and partners, we also use them with God.

Attachment Science

Attachment styles are the profiles of our basic approach to relationships. They are the pattern of how we seek and maintain closeness and connection.

How do you try to get closeness from God? That depends on your *attachment style*. Attachment styles are the profiles of our basic approach to relationships. They are the pattern of how we seek and maintain closeness and connection, and they tend to be consistent over the course of our lives. It's an aspect of our personality that impacts how we relate to our parents, spouses, children, God, and anyone else who is important to us.

We all have ways that we reach for closeness that wear us out rather than bringing the peace and rest we've been promised. These are called "insecure" attachment styles, and they tend to fall into three distinct categories:

- an anxious attachment style
- a shutdown attachment style
- a shame-filled attachment style

Understanding your attachment style helps you look at the "maps" you've been given for closeness and why they either work out or wear you out. There are hundreds of maps, but they all tend to fall into these three attachment styles. In discovering your attachment style, you can uncover how your specific needs can point you toward a healthier path of seeking God.

An anxious attachment style of spirituality is a way of desperately trying to keep close to God. It can look different from person to person, but it could look like the person who hopes their passionate worship will bring a sense of intimacy, or who rigidly keeps a prayer time for fear of losing touch with God, or who tries to impeccably follow God. They feel that the weight of maintaining the relationship falls squarely on their shoulders, and while they are emotionally open with God, they also constantly worry about the state of their spirituality.

A shutdown attachment style of spirituality is a way of relating to God that conquers feelings. In this style, faith is more important than feelings, and building a framework of theological knowledge is the bedrock of connection with God. Emotions have little room in this way of relating to God, and holding the correct beliefs becomes a way to bypass around grief, worry, and other uncomfortable emotions that are part of the human experience.

A *shame-filled attachment style* is grounded in the feeling that God loves us but doesn't really like us. Since we've fallen so far below God's standard of perfection, we shame and blame ourselves for being so unlovable, even though God has chosen to love us. We even try to get close to God by proving that we truly know how bad and unlovable we are. We know that God will have mercy on us if we beat ourselves up enough.

Each of these styles has its own strengths and its own logic, though they can be hard to see from the outside. Plus, each summary is just the tip of the iceberg of each style. On the following page, you can take an assessment to find out which of these attachment styles of spirituality you tend toward most.

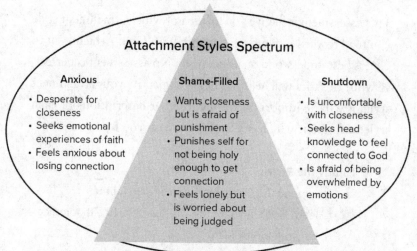

Attachment Styles Spectrum

Anxious
- Desperate for closeness
- Seeks emotional experiences of faith
- Feels anxious about losing connection

Shame-Filled
- Wants closeness but is afraid of punishment
- Punishes self for not being holy enough to get connection
- Feels lonely but is worried about being judged

Shutdown
- Is uncomfortable with closeness
- Seeks head knowledge to feel connected to God
- Is afraid of being overwhelmed by emotions

Everyone finds themselves on this spectrum sometimes. Shame-filled spirituality fits in the middle because you're both desperate for closeness and uncomfortable with it, embodying elements of both anxious and shutdown attachment styles. If you feel far from God, it's helpful to ask, "Am I relating to God with anxious, shutdown, or shame-filled attachment style right now?"

Keep in mind that you may use all three styles at different times. Each person has a specific profile and inhabits a particular point on a spectrum between these three types of attachment styles.

Understanding what attachment style is most prominent for you will help you identify what spiritual practices might help you feel closer to God. This movement toward God, this feeling of closeness, is part of a *secure attachment*. In the next chapter, we'll define secure attachment and discuss what it looks like to reach for closeness in healthy ways, based on your attachment style.

WHAT'S *YOUR* ATTACHMENT STYLE?

This assessment will give you an idea of which attachment style you tend toward in your relationship with God. Attachment to God is best understood on a spectrum. No assessment is perfect, so while this tool will help you begin to identify your attachment style, it will be important to read further descriptions of each style to find out which one resonates with you most.

1. **I study the Bible . . .**
   a. to understand God's message or plan for me.
   b. to learn God's plan for the world and build a theological framework for my faith.
   c. to make sure I am obeying God and not sinning.
2. **At church (in the present *or* past) others experience me most as . . .**
   a. vulnerable and authentic.

b. reliable and helpful.

c. quiet and shy.

3. **I believe spiritual growth comes *most* from . . .**

a. spending time with God in prayer or meditation.

b. learning about God through studying the Bible.

c. rigorous accountability to others.

4. **What I find most compelling about Jesus's life is . . .**

a. God made it possible for us to be together.

b. God fulfilled a salvation plan that began in Genesis.

c. God took the punishment that I deserved.

5. **I feel most frustrated with God . . .**

a. when God seems silent.

b. almost never. I don't usually feel frustrated with God.

c. when I feel like God sets standards for holiness I can't live up to.

6. **I feel like I fit best when . . .**

a. serving the needs of others (food bank, hospitality, maintenance team, etc.).

b. in an accountability group.

c. in a small group or Bible study.

7. **During a musical worship service . . .**

a. I love reading the truth in the lyrics.

b. I feel uncomfortable.

c. I hope to feel close to God, or I do feel close to God.

8. **God loves me . . .**

a. just like God loves everyone else.

b. because God has to love me.

c. despite the fact that I don't deserve it.

9. **My biggest concern about my relationship with God usually is . . .**

    a. Am I continuing to learn the Bible and do what's right?

    b. Have I done something wrong that's creating distance between me and God?

    c. Am I making God a big enough priority in my life?

10. **When I recognize I've sinned . . .**

    a. I know God has already forgiven me, so no need to talk to God about it.

    b. I confess, but I still feel bad.

    c. I immediately confess and ask for forgiveness.

11. **I worry most about . . .**

    a. going to hell or losing my faith.

    b. staying emotionally close with God.

    c. doing enough for the kingdom of God and the gospel.

12. **During quiet time or Bible study, I usually . . .**

    a. feel guilty, or I feel pressure to have a "spiritual experience."

    b. feel like God has a special message for me.

    c. learn things to ground my faith and worldview.

13. **When thinking about the Christian life . . .**

    a. sometimes I worry if I will ever change or grow.

    b. I'm excited about continuing to grow and become more like Jesus.

    c. I feel like I do a good job of following Jesus, but there's always room to grow.

14. **It seems like God . . .**

    a. doesn't move in me, or interact in my life, as much as in the lives of those around me.

    b. is just waiting to connect with me.

    c. likes me just as much as God likes everyone else in the world.

15. **When it comes to decisions in my life . . .**
    a. I don't feel capable of making good decisions.
    b. I ask God in prayer about nearly all of them.
    c. I make them based on my understanding of the Bible.

16. **When I follow Jesus's teaching to care for the least of these, my biggest motivation is . . .**
    a. that I am emotionally impacted by the suffering of others.
    b. to avoid God's judgment of injustice.
    c. fulfilling that part of the life of a follower of Jesus.

17. **When I think about heaven . . .**
    a. I look forward to worshiping God forever.
    b. I worry if I will fit in there.
    c. I think about what needs to be done before then, like global missions and local ministries.

18. **I feel closest to God . . .**
    a. during a musical worship service.
    b. after I've confessed my sins.
    c. learning theology or grasping truths from the Bible.

19. **When I don't have time for my regular spiritual practices . . .**
    a. I worry that I'm drifting from God.
    b. I feel like God's disappointed with me.
    c. I remind myself that my other tasks, like work and family, are important too.

20. **When I feel anxiety or sadness . . .**
    a. I ask God to help me feel better.
    b. I feel like if I really believed the Bible, then I wouldn't feel those emotions.
    c. I remind myself of biblical encouragements to "be strong and courageous" and to "rejoice in the Lord always."

Scoring Key

Tally the number of each letter for each section (noted below), then tally each column.

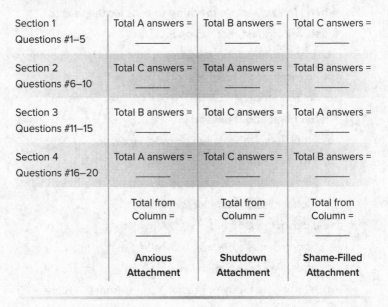

	Anxious Attachment	Shutdown Attachment	Shame-Filled Attachment
Section 1 Questions #1–5	Total A answers = _____	Total B answers = _____	Total C answers = _____
Section 2 Questions #6–10	Total C answers = _____	Total A answers = _____	Total B answers = _____
Section 3 Questions #11–15	Total B answers = _____	Total C answers = _____	Total A answers = _____
Section 4 Questions #16–20	Total A answers = _____	Total C answers = _____	Total B answers = _____
	Total from Column = _____	Total from Column = _____	Total from Column = _____

WHAT DOES MY NUMBER MEAN?

The higher the number score in each column, the more likely you tend toward that style of attachment. While this gives you a starting point, reading through the chapters on the attachment styles will help you further explore your attachment with God. Ultimately, in reading about each style, you should be able to identify which you feel best fits your style of relating to God.

Chapter Two

YOUR STYLE AND WHAT IT MEANS

What is secure attachment?

Recently, my five-year-old son was dancing on top of a chair in our kitchen. He loves dancing and, apparently, finding new places to dance. I asked him to get down. "I don't want you to hurt yourself," I said in an annoyed voice. He temporarily heeded my warning while I went into another room. Within one minute I heard a crash and immediate wailing. I walked down the hallway, but before I could even make it into the kitchen, he was running toward me, tears streaming down his face.

I picked him up and gave him a hug, and he quickly calmed down. Of course, like any parent, I felt a little frustrated because *I had just told him he would hurt himself.* But I knew we would have *that* conversation in a minute. At this moment, he simply wanted a hug from his dad who would pick him up, rock him gently, and help him calm down.

Secure attachment is a quality of relationship. It's knowing that when I need you, you'll be available, responsive, and engaged. Secure attachment happens when children can naturally turn toward their parents, or someone else they love, without much worry about whether they'll be able to get what they need. The relationship doesn't have to be perfect, but healthy connection happens often enough that we can count on that person.

A COZY CABIN

Imagine that secure attachment is a cozy cabin, and you have the key to it that you carry around in your pocket. You don't need to stay there all day, but you know that if you need some comfort, you can get into the cabin. Sometimes just slinking your hand into your pocket and feeling the key is a comfort in itself.

It's knowing that you can count on your parent to stick around and give you comfort when you're sad or scared or hurt or had a bad day. You know that if you and your parent are in a still-face moment, you won't stay there for long. Soon enough they will respond to you and give you the closeness you need. You also know that those you love will step into your emotional experience with you and respond with empathy. We find that in securely attached relationships, others rejoice with us when we rejoice and mourn when we mourn.

Lastly, in secure attachment, we feel accepted as we are. We're not just tolerated but are a delight to those who love us. Of course, healthy relationships make room for growth and boundaries, but we know the connection is not contingent on either of these, *and we can feel that stability.* In secure relationships, we know we belong in the cozy cabin, and there's no unease when we're there, no striving or earning our keep. We are delighted in for who we are, not for what we've done—or for who we could be.

Research Insight

Research suggests that to develop a healthy, secure relationship with their children, parents need to get it right only 50 percent of the time.[1] Parents don't need to be perfect, only "good enough," so there's a lot of room for error. It's estimated that 60 percent of the US population is securely attached.[2]

A SECURELY ATTACHED PRODIGAL

One of the best examples of this sort of relationship is Jesus's parable of the prodigal son. The story begins with a father and his two sons. The younger son asks for his share of the estate. Basically, the son is telling his father that he'd prefer he were dead so he can plunder the money that's coming to him. Rather than becoming offended and refusing, the father divvies up his property between the two sons, and the younger son runs away to a distant land. While there, he squanders all he has on "wild living." You can imagine your own definition of "wild living," but eventually he ends up penniless. And then something worse happens.

There's a famine in the land, and he finds himself in desperate need. Rather than returning home, he makes a last-ditch effort at taking care of himself, filling a position as a hired hand, feeding pigs—a notoriously unclean animal in Jewish society. He ends up wishing he could eat the pig food, he's so hungry. Again his needs play front and center, and the regret about how he's hurt his father seems to be part of the calculation of meeting that need. His first thought is, "My father's hired servants have food to spare, and here I am starving to death!"[3] and *then* he comes up with his apology speech. He doesn't feel guilt—initially anyway. He feels hungry.

So he returns home, prepared to give a speech about his own unworthiness, hoping to appease his father enough to get some better living conditions. But before he can even spit the words out of his mouth, while he's a long way off, his father sees him in the distance and sprints toward him. A respected man of that day would never run, especially toward a disgraced son. But this father throws dignity to the wind, wrapping the son in a huge hug, pig slop and all, and kisses him. The son says, "I am no longer worthy to be called your son,"[4] but this seems incomprehensible to the father, who immediately starts planning a welcome home party.

There is one person who agrees with the prodigal son: that he is indeed no longer worthy to be called son. It's the embittered older brother, who is furious that he himself followed the rules and received the same acceptance as his brother, who basically spit in his father's face at the beginning of the story. Scholars believe the older brother was a clear nod to the religious leaders of the day, not unlike religious leaders of our day, who tended to think of relationship worthiness in the context of what we've done or not done.

Research Insight

Research has shown that secure relationships help us get better sleep. Even when we're sleeping, our brains are assessing for emotional safety, and we rest better when we know that the relationship is secure.

In this story we see three dynamics of how the father fosters a secure relationship. First, the father's door is always open, so the son doesn't have to worry about whether he can come back and have his needs met. This means the son can explore the world, even making terrible decisions, but the father will always be there with open arms. We also see that the father is waiting to meet his son's needs. So when the son's time of need comes, he can go to the father. The father doesn't lecture him or make him feel bad. Rather, he's excited to help and support him! Finally, we see that the father doesn't hold any hard-and-fast conditions: the son doesn't have to clean himself up before he gets a hug. He's accepted as he is, and his father sees the person he loves, beneath the dirty clothes and previous snotty attitude, simply delighting in his son's presence. Jesus gave us this picture of God, a parent who provides all we need for secure relationship—even when we run far away.

DEALING WITH INSECURITIES

Just like Mother Teresa and Mr. Rogers, we all have times of feeling far from God. It's part of the life of faith. Sometimes we feel quite secure, while other times we find ourselves employing a few strategies to try to keep God close. We cut out TV time and join a Bible study that promises we'll "go really deep." We listen to more worship music. We buy a new journal, hoping to fill it with daily prayers. Sometimes these strategies work, and sometimes they don't.

In the previous chapter, I gave you a brief overview of the three attachment styles. Each of these styles tells us about the ways we try to keep connection and helps us understand specific practices that will help us build security with God, according to our particular needs. You may have noticed that while the ways we deal with disconnection can look very different from one another, they all attempt to accomplish the same goal: closeness with God. We're going to take a deeper look into each of the three styles so we can answer this question: What should I do when my connection to God feels insecure?

Anxious Attachment

Anxious attachment is a pattern of worriedly seeking closeness with God, fearing that the moment we relax, we will backslide into separation. We're convinced it's entirely up to us to maintain closeness with God, which means we can never actually rest with God. It's up to you to stay close to God through prioritizing time in prayer, regular church attendance, or scheduled Bible reading.

In some families, the child ends up feeling that keeping connection rests wholly on their shoulders, a feeling many of us have picked up in our faith communities as well. This approach to closeness prevents us from ever resting in the embrace of a loving parent and pushes us to cling anxiously to them. It's exhausting, but better than being abandoned to disconnection.

In healthy families, children trust that their parents will respond and rescue them from disconnection, at least most of the time. But what if you grew up in a family where it was more likely that your cry would be ignored than responded to? You were unsure if you'd be rescued, or if you'd feel abandoned to the utter hopelessness of isolation. It's scary to be alone in a world where no one comes to save you from the painful feeling of disconnection. So you created a pattern of frantically calling out for help and eventually focused all your energy on preventing disconnection from ever happening in the first place.

When we can't trust our caregivers to come close in our time of need, we have to scheme up our own map for closeness. We know our parents care, but we're not sure if they care *enough*. If we're skeptical that they will help us during the agony of disconnection, our best strategy becomes avoiding any distance at all. Our relationships begin to feel like helium balloons, constantly bobbing and pulling, threatening to fly away unless we grip tight the strings that hold them close.[5] It's safer to sit next to Mom on the bench at the park than take the risk of playing on the playground. What if she's not paying enough attention when you venture out on your own and become hurt or scared? The best bet is to cling to Mom's skirt and endlessly keep a sharp eye out for the slightest sign of disconnection.

Emotional Intensity

The emotional intensity of the charismatic tradition can help us quell our anxiety about God's closeness, providing a space to call out and expect that God will show up. But for some of us, as the intensity fades, the anxiety about distance increases, wearing us out over time.

When we practice an anxious attachment style, we worry about drifting, backsliding, or falling away from the faith. If we don't keep the connection, who will? Many of us were told early on in our faith that keeping God close is what the Christian life is about. Taking on all the responsibility for our connection with God, we have to double-check that we are staying close, constantly gripping the balloon string. It's easy to become locked in a pattern of being as expressive as we can in our spiritual life, trying to keep God's attention. Or we might make sure always to have a quiet time or never to miss mass, and when we can't make it, we become anxious about our connection with God.

We might commit to battling whatever sin has become our vice. As Mark Dever, president of 9Marks ministry, says, "If you're not at odds with sin, you're not at home with Jesus."[6] So we tirelessly work to make sure we're at odds with sin to stay close to Jesus. We continually scan for the tiniest fracture in our connection.

Research Insight

One study that examined connections between mental health and how we relate to God found that an anxious attachment style with God significantly predicted depression and anxiety symptoms.[7]

This attachment style has created many passionate, expressive, and devout followers of Jesus. They demonstrate that God, who wants to hold us, accepts and embraces our neediness. But for many, rather than a loving embrace, relationship with God becomes a precarious balancing act that burns us out over time.

We desperately want closeness, and we have learned that the best way to get and keep it is through anxiously grasping at those we love, including God. It's a map we've received both in our families and also from the church. We long to collapse into the lap of our Divine Parent, but we worry about relaxing too much. If the consequences are closeness or eternal separation, of course we'll engage an anxious attachment style—it's the only way we know to stay close.

Shutdown Attachment

Shutdown attachment is a pattern of trying to stuff down our negative emotions to get close to God. It is based on the presumption that emotions such as fear, sadness, pain, and doubt are incompatible with the life of faith. So we try as hard as we can not to feel these feelings, often using religious language, saying, "God is in control, so why should I worry?" Shutting down uncomfortable feelings seems like the path to becoming a person who truly trusts God.

Parents who struggle with managing their own emotions will often send subtle signals to their children that feelings are not welcome in the family. To get the closeness they need, the children learn to shut down their emotions because they've learned that their feelings *cause* the still-face moments since their parents either punish emotional expression or pull away from it. As long as the children don't share too much, they can keep the connection with their parents. In American society, this is much more likely with boys, who grow up to be men who have learned that their emotions will not be heard or embraced.

In reality, emotions are designed for connection. If you've seen Pixar's movie *Inside Out*, you've learned that if you banish sadness, you overlook its role in bringing others close: when we cry, it prompts our parents to scoop us up and give us kisses, respond with soothing tones, and hold us close. Without sadness, others wouldn't know when to come close in our times of need. Without sadness, we wouldn't know when to reach out to others.

But in a tragic turn of events, some children learn early on that the emotions God designed to bring us together actually drive their parents away. These children learn that when they cry, Mom gets angry or Dad gets uncomfortable. The best way to stay close is to lock their unsightly feelings in the basement.

If we learn that our parents aren't comfortable with emotional closeness, we will walk a tightrope of getting close but not *too* close. If we want to maintain connection, then our best strategy is to go to our room and play with blocks when we feel like we might cry. We can't risk the rejection that might come if we shed tears, so we manage our emotions ourselves and come back for closeness when we've regained composure. We can keep connection so long as we demonstrate that we're not "irrational" or "unreasonable" or "too emotional."

Then we grow into adults who hold others at a distance to keep them close, often confusing friends, partners, and ourselves. It's a paradoxical strategy. From the outside it looks like we couldn't care less about closeness, but we've learned that if we get too close, we will be pushed away. So the distance becomes a way of maintaining closeness. We avoid sharing emotions at all costs, our bodies remembering on a nonverbal level that doing so resulted in rejection by those we love most. We keep connected by shutting down emotions that might threaten closeness.

We often feel unpracticed and incompetent in the world of connecting emotionally, so we're more comfortable with activities that are shoulder-to-shoulder rather than face-to-face. We'd rather go on a bike ride with a friend than sit down for a cup of coffee. We'll show up for a building project but feel anxious when faced with unstructured social times. Church potlucks are the worst; we much prefer a cookout where at least we can manage the grill.

Lack of Emotional Intensity

The liturgy of mainline church traditions can harbor those with shutdown attachment styles because weekly worship does not necessarily require emotional engagement, in contrast to evangelical churches that put a prime emphasis on emotional worship. White Baptist and Reformed churches also often create cultures that allow us to escape into our heads, through pursuing theological knowledge, while escaping the emotions of our hearts.

Then we also practice a shutdown attachment style with God. We think having negative emotions means there's something wrong with our faith. The church sends many messages—sometimes subtle, sometimes not—that our emotions are not welcome. Kathleen Norris wrote in *The Cloister Walk* that she was raised to believe she had to "be dressed up, both inwardly and outwardly, to meet God,"[8] to "be a firm and even cheerful believer before I dare show my face in his church."[9] The fruit of the Spirit, feelings like joy and peace, indicate a true connection with God. Therefore, fear, doubt, and pain must indicate that there's something wrong with our faith.

Untangling Evangelicalism

John MacArthur declares, "Lack of joy is a sin for the child of God."[10] What does this mean for the countless Christians who struggle daily with depression?

Some of us have been taught that the very existence of certain feelings is an affront to God. Francis Chan wrote, "Worry implies that we don't quite trust God," suggesting that "both worry and stress reek of arrogance."[11] We don't want to drive God away with our foul-smelling emotions, so we come up with a handful of tools to manage them on our own. Usually this looks like some version of either working extra hard to conjure up feelings of peace and joy or shutting down altogether so we don't feel anxious or worried or happy or anything at all. We'll do whatever we can to keep God close, so we try to subdue our emotions under our control, something we were never capable of in the first place. We stuff our feelings in the basement, hoping they won't drive God away.

Untangling Evangelicalism

Oswald Chambers has written, "If through a broken heart God can bring His purposes to pass in the world, then thank Him for breaking your heart."[12] Have you ever felt like God cared more about expanding the kingdom of heaven than caring for your heart?

A shutdown attachment makes no room for needs or emotions. We get going on God's cosmic mission and forsake anything that gets in the way. It seems God cares more about fame and glory than our emotions and experience. God feels like a parent who doesn't notice we've had a bad day at school because they're so busy trying to get their own work done. Just as those with a shutdown style will choose completing a task over connecting emotionally, we find a similar portrayal of a God who is focused on the task of spreading the gospel or establishing a kingdom, without concern for feelings. In this paradigm, we've lost a vision for a God who both invites us into self-sacrificial living *and* knows us so well that the hairs on our heads are counted. Instead, God becomes a cosmic boss who cares more about the cause than being in communion together.

In shutdown attachment we find ways to connect with our faith communities that sidestep emotions. We volunteer to organize meal trains or set up for services. We lead a small group and become knee-deep in content in a way that crowds out any room for the personal parts of the community. We participate as best we can, all the while ensuring that relationships don't become too intimate.

We who practice a shutdown style of spirituality have often helped the church create systems of theology and ways of thinking about God that are a unique gift to the church. We are often good at planning and organizing ministry tasks. Our "left brain" approach has many benefits to the church and to our communities. But we can end up struggling to feel emotionally connected to others or to God.

Our relationship with God can never be the refuge we need because we can't risk crawling into the lap of a God who will find our worry to be offensive. We can't take the chance of sharing our pain or doubt or fear lest it lead to terrifying disconnection, so we squash our feelings, hoping that will keep God close. But over time, without the ability to go to God with our stress, feeling authentically connected spiritually—to God and others—becomes increasingly difficult. Our practice of shutdown attachment leave us starved for the true connection we need.

Shame-Filled Attachment

Shame-filled attachment believes that the best way to get close to God is to shame and blame ourselves for falling below the standard of perfection. We tell ourselves that if we could just be a little better, we could get close. But we can never transform quite enough, so if we can't become adequately holy, we can at least punish ourselves for not being good enough. We end up trying to get close by proving to God that we know how bad and unlovable we are.

In childhood, if we receive mixed messages about our parents' feelings toward us, we can't trust that they want closeness. One day they seem to love us, the next they seem annoyed with or outright hostile toward us. In the worst situations, we live with the threat of abuse and violence, even on the days when our parents tell us how much they adore us.

Untangling Evangelicalism

John Piper believes "it's right for God to slaughter women and children anytime he pleases."[13] It can be difficult to see God as a loving parent when we hear teachings like these.

We take this hostility to mean there is something wrong with us, something that makes us undeserving of love and closeness. So we try to become a different person, someone our parents might love more. When we can't, we end up punishing ourselves for not being someone worthy of love. This looks like the kid who continually criticizes himself in his head before his parents have a chance to. If he can find all his faults, he'll be prepared for the shame that is waiting for him as he tries to get close to his parents.

In adulthood, this attachment style makes relationships difficult to navigate. We desperately want closeness. We make our desire for connection clear to others until our shame catches up with us, and then we shut down or push others away, fearing they will see us for who we really are. We feel all alone in the world yet terrified to let anyone close.

Researchers have called this style *disorganized attachment* or *fearful attachment* because there's no clear way to seek emotional safety in the relationship. I've decided to call this way of relating shame-filled attachment because the foundation of this style is shame. It thrives on the belief that I am not good enough to deserve love and belonging.

This dynamic can play out in our relationship with God. We try desperately to scrub ourselves clean because we want to get close to God. But when that doesn't work, we try another method: we can at least hate the dirty parts of ourselves. Since there are repulsive parts of us that keep God away, we try to placate God by showing that we know how disgusting we are. We end up telling God that we understand why we don't deserve closeness.

Sin, Guilt, and Shame

Churches that constantly remind us how far we've fallen from God's ideal often implicitly or explicitly promote shame in the pews. Rather than focusing on God, they focus more on humans and their sinfulness. In the US, this is common in the recent neo-Reformed movement, but this feeling of constant disapproval has also been felt in many Catholic churches, such as the often-mentioned experience of "Catholic guilt."

We regularly hear shame-filled messages in the church. We know that because of our sinful hearts, God is repulsed and finds us "thoroughly unpleasing when it comes to personal relationship," as John Piper put it.[14] God delights in us only when we become someone slightly—or wholly—different. Piper continued, "God sees the incremental advances of our transformation by his Spirit and delights in them."[15] It sounds nice, but it requires us to continually advance forward, step-by-step, for us to get the delight that we deeply desire. With a shame-filled attachment style, we can't rest in our father's arms covered in pig slop like the prodigal son. God delights in us only *after* we change our attitude and put on fresh clothes.

Untangling Evangelicalism

The "prince of preachers," Charles Spurgeon, a revivalist in nineteenth-century England, wrote, "I feel myself to be a lump of unworthiness, a mass of corruption, and a heap of sin,"[16] referring to himself as "all rottenness, a dunghill of corruption, nothing better and a great deal worse."[17] Do we have to feel this way about ourselves before we can come to God?

Since becoming a different, more lovable person is difficult, we resort to hating the person we are today, hoping God will see that at least we know we've fallen short. So throughout the day, we keep a list of everything we've done wrong and how badly we've screwed up in response to God's grace. In a shame-filled attachment style, feeling bad becomes a mark of closeness. Former president of the Southern Baptist Convention J. D. Greear said, "One of the surest signs that you've never met God is that you feel pretty good about yourself."[18] This means *either* that getting close to God requires feeling bad about yourself first or that getting close to God causes you to feel bad about yourself. With our attachment glasses on, we can clearly see that neither of these is a sign of a healthy relationship.

Untangling Evangelicalism

Five hundred years ago, John Calvin wrote, "There is no reason why we should feel safe when God declares himself opposed to and angry with us,"[19] and this message continues to reverberate in the church to this day. How do you make sense of God's anger in Scripture?

A shame-filled attachment style puts us in a terrible place where we feel better when we're distant from God and feel worse about ourselves when we're close. Yet we need closeness, so we're caught in a terrible dilemma. Though we long to draw near to God, as we come closer, we can see only disgust in the eyes of the Divine. We experience a nettling feeling that we need to become a bit better, a little holier, for God to like us. And if that doesn't work, we can acknowledge outright that we aren't lovable and don't expect true closeness until we've completely changed.

Attached to God

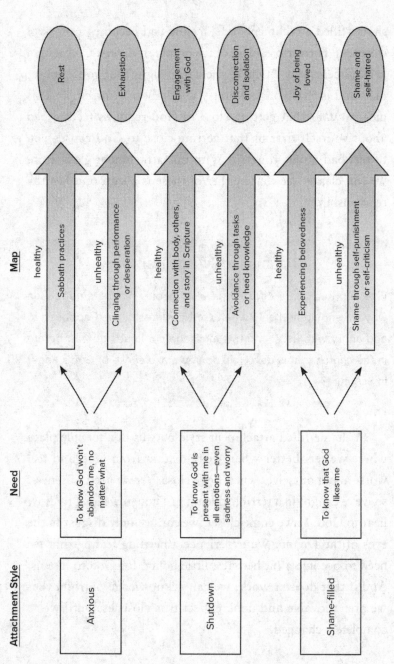

Those of us with a shame-filled attachment style often understand, in a visceral way, the gravity of being human, as well as the magnitude of connection with the Divine. We can create spaces in the church that allow for brokenness and admission of failures. But we often feel like there's no true way to connect with God, so long as we're as defective as we feel.

With a shame-filled attachment style, there is no immediate solution to the closeness we need. We find ourselves vacillating between judgmental nearness and lonely distance. We've lost the vision of a Father who delights in us, and in so doing, also lost a vision of ourselves as children of God, dearly loved. Because of this dynamic, we are stuck with both the longing for closeness and the discomfort of being close, just like a shut-down attachment style. It is not only confusing but can also be incredibly painful.

The graphic on the previous page is a picture of what you'll learn in this book. As you identify your attachment style, you will also see the emotional need that you have and some of the healthy and unhealthy ways you may try to meet that need.

BEYOND CATEGORIES

It's important to remember that you will not fit squarely in one style. Reading through the styles of spirituality, you likely resonated with at least a couple of styles, if not all—including the cozy cabin of secure attachment. My friend Jeffrey Olrick says, "Categories are for research, not for people."[20] Everyone is on the attachment spectrum, somewhere between anxious, shutdown, and shame-filled. Each person has a specific profile. We each learn different approaches and skills to get closeness. As you read, you may resonate with parts of each chapter. That's normal —and exactly what I confusingly found for myself when I first started reading descriptions of different attachment styles. That's because each of us uses all the strategies at one point or another.

Therapeutic Insight

A note for the parents reading: as we dig into these styles of relating, looking at the impact that parents have can cause anxiety, guilt, or paralyzing shame. But remember, you only need to be a "good enough" parent. You don't have to be perfect to develop a deep connection with your children. We all have natural strengths when it comes to parenting, as well as aspects that we will continue working on for the rest of our lives as parents.

It's also very important to recognize that each kid has their own temperament. Some kids are more anxious, and it's not related to attachment. There are genetic components that impact the way our kids approach the world. While attachment science is a helpful way to understand the "how and why" of our patterns for approaching relationships, it's not the whole picture, especially when it comes to our child's mental health and personality.

Rather than trying to assess your child's attachment, pick up a book to learn more about connecting with your child. Here are some helpful attachment-based books can give you concrete tips to increase the secure bond between you and your child.

- *The 6 Needs of Every Child* by Amy and Jeffrey Olrick
- *The Whole-Brained Child* by Daniel J. Siegel and Tina Payne Bryson

- *The Connected Child* by Karyn Purvis, David R. Cross, and Wendy Lyons Sunshine
- *Raising a Secure Child* by Kent Hoffman, Glen Cooper, and Bert Powell

Additionally, experts have found that when parents do the work to understand their own attachment styles, it increases their ability to be responsive to their children. While looking at your own approach to relationships can feel overwhelming, when we do so, it benefits not only us but also those entrusted to our care.

This chapter is only the beginning of understanding each of these attachment styles. Each style deserves a closer look, which you will find in the following three chapters, each dedicated to one of the three attachment styles. Feel free to skip to yours first, but learning about each style can help you better relate to others in your life who have a different attachment style than you.

As we dig into each style, not only will you understand the motivations of each style and what they look like, you will also see how your style impacts the way you relate to others, yourself, and God. Most importantly, you'll learn practices to foster feelings of closeness and security with God, based on your specific style and your particular God-given needs.

Chapter Three

ANXIOUS SPIRITUALITY

Have you ever been in a relationship with someone clingy? Like, can't-catch-a-breath, stuck-to-your-side sort of clingy? I don't mean someone who celebrates half-year anniversaries and leaves love notes in your lunch every day. I mean someone who requires you to constantly field a barrage of text messages; places day-in, day-out demands on your attention; and expects that most, if not all, nights will be spent together. It's an exhausting assignment: constantly trying to reassure your partner, walking on eggshells, and making sure they know that the relationship is solid.

Or perhaps you are the clingy person. Under the right circumstances, we all have the propensity to become suffocatingly clingy. As a couples therapist, I've seen boomer-generation men who have spent their whole lives swimming alone in the cultural streams of individualism go through a tectonic life change and suddenly become as needy as a lovestruck teenager in their first relationship.

If you've felt this desperate never-ending need for reassurance, you know what it's like to live with an anxious attachment style. You also know something that can be hard to see from the outside: being the clingy one is even more exhausting than it is to be clung to. Let me explain.

You're five years old, and the sun is hot, and barnyard smells waft through the air, tickling your nose. It's the county fair, mid-July, and your grandparents just bought you a red balloon with your favorite cartoon character on it. It bobs and tugs, threatening to fly away into the bright blue sky at any moment.

The first order of business, as soon as money was exchanged, was to tie it around your wrist. But at five years old, you have a hard time trusting that the tie is going to hold, so with white knuckles, you grip the string in your little hands all afternoon. The sweat makes the already-too-thin curling ribbon slide through your fingers, so you constantly have to pull it back down, ensuring that it doesn't get too far away. About two feet above your head feels like a comfortable distance, which happens to be at the level of bumping all the adults' faces, but letting it go any higher makes you nervous.

You spend the afternoon eating corn dogs, sliding down slides on burlap sleds, watching a hypnotist show, and looking at animals. All the while, your attention is always split, with a little allocated to ensuring the balloon isn't slipping from your hands. It's hard to be fully present, to explore the fair and notice everything, with your mind on the balloon. It's better than losing the balloon, but it's also exhausting in a way that's almost hard to put your finger on.

WHITE-KNUCKLE CLOSENESS

If you cannot trust those you love to stick around, then you are left with only one guaranteed strategy to keep the closeness you desire: *you* have to keep them close. Of course, this doesn't show up only in relationship to God. There are a lot of ways you might clutch tightly to the different relationships in your life. You might send one—or ten—too many text messages. You might demand to be with your partner as much as possible to stave off the worry that fills you when you're apart. Or you try to earn your keep in the relationship, like making breakfast every morning for your spouse or meeting up for coffee dates at times that are convenient for your friend but not for you. You might continually test the connection, like walking into the other room to see how long it takes before someone misses you, or pushing others away to see if they still bounce back.

You constantly monitor the distance, alert to any signs of disconnection. There are various ways to try to keep others close: quietly people-pleasing, never saying no when you should, or angrily demanding attention when you feel a rupture in the relationship. It could also look like constantly asking for reassurance, always telling yourself, *I just need to know we're okay.* Underneath all these behaviors is the same anxiety telling you that the moment you relax your grip, you will lose connection—and the balloon will go flying off into the sky.

EARLY STRATEGIES

If a child grows up with parents who respond inconsistently to their needs, they learn to approach relationships with anxiety. These types of parents are well-intentioned but often fail to tune in to their child. During times when the child needs attention, the parents are caught in their own world, while times when he is happy to play alone, they interrupt and engage in a way that doesn't fit the moment. Of course, all parents do this at times, but when parents are unattuned more often than not, it creates unpredictability for the child. This makes the child feel that he can't rely on his parents for connection when he really needs it. In the still-face moments, it feels like his parents are out of reach, like a balloon high in the sky.

As the child tries to figure out the rhyme and reason to these patterns, he creates his own solution: *if I can constantly keep them close, I won't find myself in a still-face moment in the first place.* In childhood, this looks like physical closeness or becoming very upset the moment his parents' attention is elsewhere. It's like when kids repeatedly say, "Mom, watch me!" except 24/7. Or it could be a child who lurks near Mom, afraid to stray too far and feel all alone. The anxious infant eventually resorts to tightly gripping his mother's skirt, for fear she will disappear if he doesn't cling.

When he does find himself in a still-face moment, he gets attention the only way he knows how: he gets loud, demonstrative, or dramatic, sending up a flare that pulls his parents into his orbit when needed. It's the only thing that gets his unreliable parents' attention. Then he grows up and tends to exaggerate his needs and feelings while at the same time expecting he won't be heard. This strategy helped many of us survive childhood. But this pattern of relating tends to overwhelm or exhaust those around us in adult life, often leading them to pull away, the very thing we fear most.

INTERNAL ALARMS

When my wife and I first moved to Minneapolis, we lived in an apartment complex once known as "the pit." After a change in ownership, the building manager partnered with nonprofits in the area to provide housing to people who would otherwise have difficulty finding housing. The community shifted and created more safety than there had been. But it was still a run-down place. We literally had anthills coming up out of the carpet at one point. Despite that fact, the worst part of the apartment was the smoke alarm.

Every time we cooked, it would set off the wired-in smoke detector. Eventually, the only way we knew how to cook in peace was to cook in the dark. We had to flip the circuit breaker to deactivate the detector—which also turned off the kitchen lights. The detector was so sensitive to any potential threat, it would run all day if we let it. So we turned it off and plugged in a nearby lamp that provided just enough light to see the food we were cooking.

The best way I can think to describe living with an anxious attachment style is like having that smoke detector inside—an alarm that is on constant alert for the slightest sign of disconnection. Any microexpression or slight change in tone is a sign that there's a problem with the relationship. You keep hawkeyed surveillance on body language, voice, and facial expressions, trying to search for any possible signs of disappointment or rejection.

Research Insight

Research shows that people with an anxious attachment style are quicker to pick up on facial expressions and emotional cues than others.[1]

As long as there aren't any threats to the relationship, you feel safe. But that requires continually investigating and eradicating any perceived threats because in intimate relationships, the threat to connection registers in your brain as a literal threat to your safety. There's a clue that something might be wrong with your relationship, and suddenly it's impossible to think of anything else. So your brain prioritizes reestablishing connection over all else, preventing you from focusing on other matters until you have a sense of connection again. It's like a blaring alarm that can be turned off only once the fire department has come, explored the whole building, and confirmed that there is in fact no fire.

The alarm gets set off so easily that you go through the routine several times a month—or several times a day. You explore and investigate all the rooms of the relationship to make sure there isn't a pile of smoldering coals in some back corner, threatening to burn down the whole building. Your partner poorly phrases a comment, and you shoot back, "What did you mean by that?" already anticipating the disconnection. Or if you're an internal processor, you hear the remark and ruminate day and night about what they might have meant. It's a constant internal monologue that asks, *Are we okay? Are we okay? Are we okay?*

Psychological Insight

Living under the constant threat of disconnection can create numerous physiological problems. This continual threat of losing closeness can cause increased blood pressure, gastrointestinal problems, poor sleep, and many other ways our bodies respond to feeling unsafe.

These ways of anxiously checking our connections can feel tiresomely needy to those closest to you. Continually on the lookout for signs of rejection, you soak up reassurance like a sponge and become prickly in its absence. You always have to check to see if the relationship is as solid as it seems. Carefully attuned to any cracks in the foundation, you have a tendency to become scared quickly, and then angry, about anything that looks like a tiny fracture.

PURSUING GOD

Obviously, being too focused on relationships in our lives can wear on us—and those we love. But is it possible to focus too much on your relationship with God? How can you tell the difference between fervent devotion and frantic insecurity? How do you distinguish between secure spirituality and an anxious attachment style? If you think about it, church history is full of spiritual heroes who focused on God above all else. Scripture encourages us to hold God in mind. It becomes a little part of our conscience, always running in the background. It's almost like we are told to be anxious about our relationship with God, and we venerate those who successfully cling to God their whole lives. One such person is A. W. Tozer.

"People generally die the way they have lived," says my father-in-law, reflecting on his ministry as a hospice chaplain. Tozer was no exception to the rule. Arriving at the end of the life he had spent pursuing God, A. W. Tozer found himself all alone, except for the God he'd so fervently sought.

Aiden Wilson Tozer, known by most as A. W. Tozer, led a generation of Christians to understand relationship with God in a new way. His book *The Pursuit of God*, published in 1948 and now considered a Christian classic, taught believers to engage in a genuine and personal relationship with God. While Tozer's ministry was known throughout the country and the world, he was not on a quest for fame, power, or finances. He didn't desire Christian celebrity status. Rather, it was the experience of "God's pleasure" he felt while preaching that drove his ministry, which explains why he would often withdraw from the congregation after preaching, avoiding "the praise of men."

Most days he spent several hours in prayer, often prostrate. He even had a pair of "prayer pants" so he wouldn't wear out the knees of his entire wardrobe as he spent countless hours in a state of deep intimacy with God. Sometimes church staff would accidentally disrupt his prayers when they walked into his office and found him lying on the ground, weeping or moaning, deep in communion with the Holy Spirit. He wrote poetry and praises, obsessed with all sorts of romantic writing about God. Tozer lived in the cloud of connection I so desperately wanted as a teenager.

A life of simplicity was a primary part of Tozer's singular devotion to God. After receiving his salary from churches, he would often return half of it as a donation back to the church and consistently refused pay raises from church boards. After his books gained popularity, he reassigned royalties to benefit various ministry organizations. With a mind to stay focused on what was most important, he wanted to ensure that treasures of the world could not distract him, denying even basic conveniences like a car. His goal was clear: to satiate his increasingly consuming "hunger after God himself."[2] Tozer's solitary focus was an example that ignited a fire among Christians, leading thousands to experience a relationship with God in a new, genuine way. From the outside, Tozer seemed like an avid practitioner of healthy spirituality, and it is only the witnesses of those closest to him, accounts we will soon discuss, that might make us take a second look.

EXHAUSTING PURSUIT

We've all been taught ways to pursue God. In my evangelical upbringing, I was supposed to have a daily quiet time and think of God with every action I took throughout the day. In Catholicism, pursuing God can look like ticking all the boxes, engaging in all the sacraments and services. In charismatic circles, pursuing God means having enough faith, gathering enough belief within yourself to see God work and move. During my time in the Mennonite church, sticking close to God meant remaining in community and living out the values of God's upside-down kingdom, which often had political implications. In other mainline traditions, some retain their relationship with God through showing up at services, engaging in liturgy and other practices. In reformed traditions, it tends to be the pursuit of learning theology that will stand the test of time. And in most Christian traditions—even among the unchurched—doing your best not to sin is a common method for getting or staying close to God. We all try to keep the balloon from flying away.

Untangling Evangelicalism

Charles Spurgeon wrote, "The Christian life is very much like climbing a hill of ice. You cannot slide up, nay, you have to cut every step with an ice axe; only with incessant labor in cutting and chipping can you make any progress."[3] How can you ever have times of rest in a faith like that?

Without the foundational belief that we are loved and accepted, it's only natural to strive to keep God close. For many, life with God is as stressful as it is soothing. Ed Cyzewski calls American Christianity "an anxiety factory"[4] in which we often worry about doing enough. No one knows this better than those of us with an anxious attachment style, always wondering, "Is my relationship with God okay? Am I doing enough?" Some deal with anxiety through the pursuit of exciting spiritual experiences, while others keep a close eye on their behavior to avoid disappointing God. Some excessively focus on "exactly right" theology—all different ways of grasping the balloon.

Psychological Insight

Researchers have suggested that an anxious attachment style would result in "clingy, dependent and inconsistent religious involvement."[5]

The problem with anxious attachment is that the more you strive for closeness with God, the less secure you feel.

You might feel *closer* but not any less worried. The longer you cling to the balloon, the more you believe it would fly away if you loosened your grip for a millisecond. You never get a chance to experience God's unfailing love if you're always focused on keeping connection. You deeply value the emotional worship service experience on Sunday, and then throughout the week you feel like you slowly starve until you can return to that place of connection. You faithfully engage in your spiritual routines and feel close to God—confirming that without them, you would feel far away. From the outside, an anxious attachment style can look like a particular holiness, and it can be hard to see the insecurity beneath. Always alert to possible rupture of relationship, you end up white-knuckling your spiritual life.

By zealously trying to keep God close, you end up deprived of the opportunity to experience the steadfast love you are promised. As with a trust fall, letting go and expecting that you'll fall into an embrace requires faith. Without a foundation of God's acceptance, the times that you do relax a little, it suddenly feels like you're falling through the air. You might even be terrified that you're backsliding, on your way to losing the faith. You engage in accountability groups or small groups or Bible studies not merely for the sake of community and health but to prevent doing something that might cause a major disconnection from God. Rather than falling into the arms of a loving God, you're terrified that you'll fall into the deep pit of apostasy. And others only affirm the feeling. When you stop your spirituality practices, others often question your relationship with God. It all works together to keep you anxiously grasping at God, hoping the relationship doesn't float away.

It can be difficult to tell whether it is fear or love that is driving your spiritual practices. Your practices become anxious only when God's presence seems dependent on engaging in these routines. It's when you worry that in the absence of these practices, God will withdraw. During a significant life transition, like having a newborn baby, your spiritual practices might have to shift. Do you worry that there's a distance creeping in? Like the balloon is slipping from your hands?

When you sin—an inevitable part of life—do you worry that it will drive a wedge in your relationship with God? When you keep doing the same stupid thing over and over again, are you scared that God is fed up with you? Do you anxiously confess in order to appease a God who is just waiting for a reason to withdraw? Do you feel worried, like this fragile relationship is slipping away? Can you trust that God is still near and cares for you during those times?

Psychological Insight

Religious obsessive compulsive disorder (OCD), also known as scrupulosity, is a mental health disorder in which someone ruminates on their relationship to God, salvation, or other spiritual-themed concerns. It can look like constantly questioning your behavior or theology, panicking that your theology isn't sufficient to save you from hell, or worrying that your behavior means you will be cut off from God forever. The line between OCD and certain religious teachings that emphasize constant religious vigilance is unclear to some clinicians.[6] Visit Jaimie Eckert's website at Scrupulosity.com to learn more about religious OCD.

The church has often allowed anxious spirituality to fly under the radar, drastically emphasizing holding God close through engaging in spiritual behaviors and avoiding sinful behaviors. Perfectionism is one of the sharpest tools in the toolbox of anxious attachment. If you can avoid mistakes, you can avoid abandonment. Many Christian practices create ecosystems for perfectionism to grow, because on the surface the effort appears to flow from a deep relationship with God. While this spiritual insecurity can feel like a constant knot in your stomach, it may often bring applause from a church community. You always show up to Bible study having completed all the homework and with the best insights. You volunteer for three ministries at your church. You regularly read books about growing closer to God. You appear to be devout—and you are. But this devotion is driven by an underlying feeling that without spiritual activities, the connection will evaporate. Without regular routines, you doubt that God will stick around.

How can you ever find respite in a spiritual life that requires you to constantly cling for closeness? My daughter used to use this tactic all the time with me. When she was scared, she would grasp my neck—nearly choking the life out of me with her tiny little arms—unable to relax into my embrace. It was less like I was holding her and more like she was clinging to a rock-climbing wall. Only after I reassured her that I wouldn't let go—no matter what—could she relax and let me hold her.

Whether it's a rock-climbing wall or a balloon ribbon or a God you can't see, constantly clinging to something is exhausting. But sadly, when you engage in an anxious attachment style, you are doing exactly what you've learned to do. You relentlessly pursue God in the way you've been taught, deprived of the opportunity to experience his unending faithfulness.

CLINGING TO GOD'S SKIRT

When it comes to anxiously attached children, it's not the child's need for closeness that's the problem—it's that she can't depend on closeness. To get what she needs, she has to divert her energy and attention away from the rest of life. Her fervency for closeness robs her of the ability to explore, grow, learn, and make new relationships. Her preoccupation with closeness keeps her from crawling across the room and trying out a new toy. Worried that her mother won't be there when she needs her, she is forced to give a large portion of her attention to measuring whether her mother is close. Maintaining connection with her mother becomes a full-time job, so she misses the opportunity to fully learn and grow. Unfortunately, this same theme plays out in the life of faith when we engage in anxious attachment patterns.

We're only as needy as our unmet needs. [7]
—Dr. John Bowlby

Let's take a closer look at the life of A. W. Tozer. It seems that Tozer's desperate need for closeness with God made it difficult for him to focus on much else, coming at a cost to those closest to him. Tozer kept a distance from his wife and was generally unavailable to most of his seven children. In one biography of Tozer, it's lamented that "the Tozer boys said they experienced very little, if any, true affection from their father."[8] While Tozer spoke of his intimacy with God, there was little left for his friends or family, who were all kept at arm's length.

His passion for a simple life had untoward consequences for his family. The choice to go without a car meant that his wife, Ada, would often ask other church members for rides around town or else brave the cold Chicago streets. His refusal to take raises meant she made do with a limited income, cooking meals that lacked nutritional value. Two of his sons said they could go the rest of their lives without eating another meal of macaroni and cheese. While Tozer made time for extended prayer daily, he only once planned a family vacation. On that single vacation, his daughter remembers that he was irritable and distracted, which might hint at a possible a discomfort with spending prolonged time with his family in contrast to his regular contemplative routine.

Then, at the end of his life, Tozer found himself in the hospital. The evening of his death he insisted that Ada go home and rest, a regular move when he was sick. No friends or children stayed overnight with him in the solitary hospital room. The only one present in his last moments was God, with whom he had enjoyed such intimacy his whole life.

Is it possible to focus *too* much on your relationship with God? It is a striking comment from Ada that brings me back to the question. Sometime after Aiden Tozer's death, she remarried a man named Leonard Odam. When asked about her new relationship, she told multiple people, "I have never been happier in my life. Aiden loved Jesus Christ, but Leonard

Odam loves me."[9] Ada suffered from her husband's spiritual life for several decades, and the harm it caused both her and her children is indisputable.

We can't truly know what drove Tozer's spiritual practices, but we can see that his choice to give his undivided attention to God cost him his ability to focus on much else. It's as though he clung to the hem of God's skirt, unable to venture out into the world, robbed of the ability to grow, learn, and engage with others.

THE GOSPEL OF GETTING CLOSE

Anxious attachment has infiltrated the way we talk about relationship with God in the church. We use "close to God" as a euphemism for acting righteously, often encouraging one another to "stay close with God" during the week, and speak of sinful patterns of behavior as being "far from God" or "walking away from God." We are told that sin separates us from God, so we feel the only way to keep him close is to make sure we never sin.

Theological Insight

Can we lose our faith? A centuries-long debate has raged in the church about this dilemma. Some believe we ultimately choose for ourselves (free will), while others believe God chooses for us (predestination). In my experience, neither position protects against the *anxiety* of falling away from the faith.

The impact of this wrong belief is that those who desperately need to know that God is near cannot be sure of that nearness, especially in their hardest times. One clear example is the way we've equated sobriety with being close to God and active addiction as being far from God. Someone might say, "With each day of sobriety, I get one step closer to God." It only makes sense, the way we talk about living righteously as being "close to God" and living sinfully as being "far from God." But the harmful yet subtle message that comes through is that God is not present when you're at rock bottom. You have to pull yourself up out of the gutter to get close to God. It's entirely up to you to keep God close. You can grasp the balloon, so long as you can stay sober. But what about when you can't seem to stay sober? What about when you keep relapsing and all you need to know is that God is near? But you've been told, in many ways, that God likes you when you're good and withdraws when you are bad.

Isn't this the toxic theology that Jesus came to turn on its head? It was generally understood that God's presence was at the center of the temple, and only certain people were allowed in. Then Jesus showed up and ate with sinners and tax collectors and prostitutes and those who were not ritually cleansed. Nothing stops God from coming close, especially not sin. Rather, the whole story of Scripture seems to show us that sinning is a surefire way to get God to show up—but we'll get to that later.

It's important to see the ways that the anxious attachment framework is embedded in our very language. When we use "close to God" as a euphemism for living righteously, it only reaffirms the belief that our connection with God depends on our behavior.

One of my clients, April, used another common way of trying to get the closeness she longed for from God. She wanted to understand God and the divine plan for her life. She would pore over Scripture each morning, filling the margins with notes, in a constant search for God's personal messages for her. She noticed that she was by far the most engaged person at any small group or Bible study she attended. She had a sense that if she put enough work into analyzing Scripture, she would find a closeness with God.

And she often did. She'd find a biblical truth that resonated deeply and felt like it was tailor-made for her life. It felt like God was speaking to her in a personal way. She would log it in her journal, and then, quickly enough, that feeling would fade. She was always trying to outrun complacency, which she was sure would cause distance from God. She had a nagging feeling that God always had something new for her to learn, a feeling that was resolved only when she kept digging deeper into Scripture. She'd been in this pattern for her whole adult life, and it made sense. Everyone in her community, including her spiritual leaders, told her that engaging in God's Word was how to connect with God. It would deliver the feelings of closeness but required the cost of constant analyzing and study. She kept it up for years, striving for closeness with God.

FALLING ASLEEP IN THE EVERLASTING ARMS

An important, deep need is at the core of the anxious attachment style. Behind your constant clinging is a deep need for a Divine

Parent who is close and unwavering. You need a relationship you can count on. Really, you want to know that God's not going anywhere, which is exactly why you cling as tight as you can. Don't we all want someone to stick around, even when we can't seem to get anything right—*especially* when we can't seem to get it right?

Many couples I work with seem to think that healthy relationships are built on perfectionism. If I always speak to my partner in just the right way, or if I learn the right words to say in the midst of conflict, or if I'm never a burden and I keep my side of the closet neat, then we'll maintain connection. But we long for closeness that is deeper than getting everything right all the time. "Getting it right" never meets our deep need to relax into the arms of a loved one. because the real way we keep closeness is not by performing but by expressing our needs and receiving a caring response. We all need someone who races toward us and embraces us before we even have the chance to explain ourselves.

In a tradition different from mine, and in an era closer to my parents' generation, Catholic priest Henri Nouwen wrote about a type of spirituality I was familiar with, a "banner-waving type of Christianity" that demanded that a person fight fiercely through the world, giving "utmost efforts" to remain close to God. But Nouwen noticed a spiritual need underneath our determined conviction. He noticed that we want to "surrender in the soft caressing hands of an understanding God."[10] Using childhood imagery, he described our desire for a secure relationship, that we might "fall asleep in safe arms, to cry without fear, to let go, relax [our] tense muscles and rest long and deep"[11] with God.

Pause for a moment and notice how it might feel for your

body to relax like that with God. It's in this kind of relationship that we find the cozy cabin, a refuge in times of trouble and when we're exhausted and lonely. We don't need to stay there all the time, but we do need rhythms of rest to break up the times of effort.

When we recognize that this need to relax into the arms of God is what drives all our clinging, we can seek God in new ways that lead us to feel close, connected, and secure. We can engage in healing practices that respond to this deep need to know that nothing can separate us from the love of God.

THE FORGOTTEN MEANING OF SABBATH

For many of us, anxiously clinging to God is the core of Christianity, so we have no idea how to do it differently. It's easy to find ourselves in a terrible dilemma: Do I continue to strive for God's closeness, or do I give up? There doesn't seem to be much room for any other way of relating to God. It feels impossible to trust-fall into the everlasting arms of an invisible God.

Returning to the story of Scripture, we see that the very rest we long for has been offered all along. When God first brought the Israelites out of Egypt, Sabbath was instituted—a time to cease striving. Old Testament scholar Walter Brueggemann noted that rest is what was supposed to distinguish Israel from the other nations of the day.[12] The people took a break to be present with one another and with God every seven days.

Sadly, "the Lord's Day" has become another time of striving. We've forgotten that God created Sabbath as a time for people to rest, not as a day to work harder at giving him glory. It often becomes a time of clinging. In many churches that have put a supreme emphasis on *personal* relationship with God, maintaining and monitoring that connection is the entire goal of church life. The Lord's Day becomes a day to do your best clinging.

This differs starkly from God's vision for rest. Indigenous theologian Randy Woodley points out that God built this rhythm of rest and exploration into the twenty-four-hour cycle: "The night dusk comes to softly compel all creation to enter into rest."[13] God wants us to take up the easy yoke, but that's hard to do when we think we're the ones responsible for God's closeness.

In case there's any confusion, Jesus himself said, "The Sabbath was made for man, not man for the Sabbath."[14] God set aside a day for rest not so we could prove our love but out of the desire to give us a break. It is in times of rest that we build secure relationships. Yet many of us have never learned how to be present with God in a restful way. Sabbath has always centered on getting closer, hearing a word, learning something new, receiving conviction, or reflecting on whether you're walking with God. It's always a time of self-assessment, which isn't true rest. So if we've never learned how to rest with God, where do we start?

PRACTICING SABBATH

How do you spend time with God out of love rather than out of fear? The traditions we have exist for a reason. Prayer is key to the Christian life. Perhaps you don't need to change your actions as much as your approach. What if—like Sabbath—prayer was for you, not for God?

In the tradition I grew up in, I was taught that prayer was either making requests or proving my devotion. Often prayer was a way of keeping God close. For us to be close, God needed to see that I was giving my time and attention to the relationship. I needed to get my "marching orders," be convicted of sins I couldn't see myself, or hear from God about my day-to-day purpose.

It wasn't until my midtwenties that I was introduced to contemplative prayer. While it can be a broad umbrella, contemplative prayer is an ancient practice of being still to increase one's awareness of God. Since it's about experiencing God's love, we don't need to do any proving or striving or make any effort at all. We only need to commit some time to the basic practice.

Deep breathing helps calm our nervous systems, helping us concretely step out of striving. Like the end of hot summer days when my son collapses on my lap and stares into space, I don't put any pressure on myself but simply relax into the presence of a God who is always there. Since God is already available, right next to me, there's nothing I need to do. By breathing deeply and choosing *not* to go back into spiritual striving, I am practicing trust. And when I find myself pleading with God to come close, I notice it, then come back to my breath.

Breathing Prayer Exercise

1. Sit in a quiet place. Rock forward and back, right and left to find a comfortable position.
2. Focus on your breath, but let it flow naturally.

3. Choose a phrase or word you can comfortably say within the time of a breath in or out. Traditionally many have used phrases like *Lord Jesus, have mercy,* but it can be as short as one word and can be a feeling you would like to experience while with God, like *safe, calm, loved,* or *peace.*

4. Set a timer on your phone. Two minutes is a fine place to start. As you breathe deeply in through your mouth and out through your nose, come back to the phrase you've chosen.

5. If your mind drifts—and it will—that's part of the process. Simply refocus.

6. After the allotted time, check in to see if your body feels any different.

7. You can do this same breathing prayer with an image instead of a word. I often imagine a baby crying on his mother's chest—a picture I was given during a particularly difficult part of my life, which I'll tell you about later. Throughout the exercise, continually bring your focus back to the image.

Breathing prayer invites your spirit into communion with God and your body into rest. It is an easy way to practice Sabbath day to day. Over time you learn in mind and body that God is present, whether you strive or you collapse. Then you can follow the rhythms God instituted, exploring during the day and resting at night. You can let go of the balloon and notice that, miraculously, it stays where it has always been.

Only when you start practicing different ways of being with God can you feel more secure. Trying something new may require the risk of a trust fall. It also might mean going against the messages you've received from many spiritual leaders in your life. Paradoxically, it is when we rest and cease our striving that we experience God's presence more consistently.

But anxious attachment is only one of three primary insecure ways we relate to God and others. We're about to look at what happens when we do the opposite of clinging. What happens when we try to keep others close by keeping them at arm's length? And how could this possibly be a strategy we use to get closeness with God?

Chapter Four

SHUTDOWN SPIRITUALITY

"I know I shouldn't feel anxious." Six little words that summarize a shutdown attachment style.

This is a phrase I've heard from countless Christians who believe that their worry or sadness or fear or traumatic pain points to one conclusion: something is wrong with their relationship with God. *If I truly believed in God's promises, then I wouldn't feel this way*, we tell ourselves. Like the childhood Sunday school song goes, "Since Jesus Christ came in and took away my sin, I'm inright-outright-upright-downright happy all the time."[1] If I'm not happy all the time, does that mean Jesus has not come in?

I wrote this book during the COVID-19 pandemic. At one point eleven churches in my state, including one from my hometown in Southern Oregon, sued the governor for the right to meet on Sunday mornings. I remember scrolling through Twitter on the day I read that news story. I saw a picture of a family, with a girl no more than ten standing in front, holding a sign made of posterboard colored with marker. "Take off your mask because God's got you covered," it read.

"Faith over fear" was the rallying cry of many of these Christians. There's that sentiment again: if you feel fear, you don't have enough faith. After all, if the fruit of closeness with God is peace and joy, then anxiety and sadness must mean there is distance in the relationship. This isn't a new view in the church. Emotions have long been taken as thermometers of our own spiritual maturity or character. If you're anxious, then you don't trust God. If you're sad, you don't believe in the resurrection. If you're lonely, you haven't spent enough time meditating on God's love. And perhaps most damaging: if you still feel the pain of trauma, you haven't fully opened yourself up to God's healing. You're in pain because you're doing it wrong.

All these negative emotions show the ways we've failed God. They mean we don't trust or don't have enough faith, or even, like Francis Chan said, that we're arrogant and prideful. All these emotions offend God, putting a wedge in the relationship. Our best strategy is to push aside these feelings, pretend they don't exist, and hope that God will stay close.

A TOUGH CHOICE: EMOTIONS OR CLOSENESS

This dynamic shows up in family relationships too. Imagine that you're four years old and running toward the playground. It's summer, so the surrounding trees are full of leaves, and the morning is early enough for the air still to be crisp. You look at the play structure and start running toward it. But before you even make it onto the mulch, you trip and your body is caught by the concrete. Your knees feel the impact, and you notice a little blood leaking out of a scrape. You feel tears well up, but you hold them back long enough to determine whether someone will respond if you let them out.

You look back at your mom, but she's already turned her face downward, immersed in a book. Looking at your life up till now, you already know how she will react if you interrupt her. She'll say she's sorry while her eyes narrow and her lips purse in annoyance, betraying her true feelings. While she says the right words, everything else tells you that she'd rather you not have these feelings. So you make a quick, subconscious decision. You decide it's better to sit with throbbing knees than to feel like a bother. Especially when you're already feeling physical pain, the subtle rejection would be too much.

You try to focus on the playground, finding something new to play with or explore. A new activity is nothing like a hug, but it's better than sitting and feeling sorry for yourself. Distraction is a second-best strategy for dealing with pain, but it's all you've got.

After a while, this process is not even a decision anymore. You know that if you're in pain, or sad or scared, your best bet is to handle it on your own. Ignore or distract. By the time you're an adult, the emotions barely register. You don't feel much, so you don't need others' help when you feel bad. You've stopped hoping that you'll get the response you truly long for. If Mom doesn't like you when you cry, it's best to stop crying—and decide that you're okay on your own.

WHEN EMOTIONS DRIVE DISCONNECTION

If our parents don't like our emotions or can't handle them, we quickly learn that the best strategy to maintain closeness is to keep our feelings under wraps. So we come up with ways to shut down our emotions.

Parents have different ways of discouraging their children from sharing emotions. "Stop crying or I'll give you something to cry about" obviously means that sadness isn't welcome. But caregivers, even with the best of intentions, often subtly send this same message. Consider the mother who can't handle her son's tears when she says he can't have candy after dinner. She swoops in, saying, "Oh, honey, don't cry!" and gives him the candy, rather than setting a healthy boundary. While the son gets what he wants, he notices that Mom isn't comfortable with his intense emotions. He learns that his emotions increase Mom's anxiety rather than bring her close. So the child is thrown into a terrible dilemma between showing emotion and maintaining connection. To avoid a still-face moment of disconnection, he does his best to stuff his emotions.

If your relationship with your parents was at all like this boy's relationship with his mom, then you too may shut down your emotions as a way of maintaining closeness. This could mean you fill your days with activities, just like the toddler on the playground. On weekends you might work around the house, plug away at a personal project, or immerse yourself in a solitary hobby, like video games or reading novels. You've learned to manage emotions by a simple strategy: ignoring them.

Without emotionally supportive caregivers, you've learned

to rely only on yourself and, in the process, have worked hard to survive. Your independence likely earns you countless rewards in a US culture that praises a rugged individualism where everyone is expected to pull themselves up by the bootstraps. Like a Clint Eastwood character, you face the day ready to single-handedly take on the world, focused on what needs to be done. You might talk about your natural distaste for emotion, claiming, "It's just who I am," or appeal to the pragmatic: "What's the point of emotions anyway?" You genuinely believe life is better when everyone stays calm. You consider yourself logical and solution-focused. Because you're not clouded by emotions, you can clearly see problems and solutions. You're the person others call when they need an urgent solution.

In the middle of solving a problem, you become frustrated with others' emotions that only seem to complicate the process. Which is where the rub happens. Your wife wants to tell you about the conflict she's having with a coworker, and from the outside, you can clearly see an easy solution. But skipping the emotions and going straight to try and solve the problem doesn't land well with her. She says doesn't want help, she wants to tell you about what it's like for her. Shutting down emotions doesn't always work when it comes to those you love.

You feel dragged down by those who cling to you and feel suffocated by the intimacy they try to push on you. Without realizing it, you often find ways to wedge a little breathing room into your relationships. While you want to keep emotions at arm's length, others feel differently. They want to know there's a human heart beating inside you, and they long to know your thoughts and feelings. A connected relationship includes feelings, which are hard to get from a robot. So a paradox happens:

you try to stay even-keeled to weather the storms of life and to keep others close. But those in your life often feel shut out by your stoicism.

LOCKED IN THE BASEMENT

"Why don't you ever open up to me?" Marie asked.

It was an interaction I've seen a million times in my office. Marie turned her gaze away from me and swiveled for full eye contact with her husband. With a flare of anger, she asked the question again, and it landed much more like an accusation: "Why don't you *ever* open up to me?" In seeming demonstration of her point, Terrell put his face in his hands.

Marie then turned away and with an exacting tone said, "I just want to know what you're feeling." She clenched her jaw in frustration, as though to indicate she wouldn't say another word until he spoke up. It was time for me to jump in.

"Terrell," I started softly, "as Marie tells you, 'I just want to know what you're feeling,'" mimicking her frustrated tone before returning to a gentle, curious voice, "right now—I'm wondering—what's going on inside you?"

"That's exactly the problem," he said quietly. "I can't tell you what's going on inside because I don't know. I can't tell you, and I can't tell her. I would if I could, but I don't even know how to understand what's going on inside."

If you have shutdown attachment, it's not exactly that you're hiding what's going on inside from others, but rather that you yourself don't know what you are feeling. Friends and family feel like you're a house with all the shades pulled, closing yourself off from the world. In reality, you're more like a glass house with a basement that's locked tight. You don't know what's down there, and you don't know how to get to it. Besides, why would you want to? It's only bad feelings down there. And even if you opened the basement, you wouldn't know what to do with those feelings! You've never had someone to help name or tame those uncomfortable feelings, so you've shut them away. It's best to force the basement door shut, leaving the mess of sensations and feelings on the other side.

So you believe, and would have others believe, that you simply aren't an emotional person. But it's not that you don't have feelings—you're just ignoring them. And ignoring emotions is not who you are; it's simply the best strategy you've come up with so far. You have much more going on under the surface than it appears from the outside, more than you may even be aware of. This aversion to emotion is a way of surviving your internal world. If you never had anyone to help you soothe your overwhelming emotions, they feel chaotic and overwhelming. Ignoring them doesn't mean they go away; it means that they're swirling around and you don't know how to process or talk about them. So you have to figure out how to manage them on your own. You distract yourself in a variety of ways, doing your best to pretend they aren't there.

HEALTHY EMOTIONAL CONNECTION

When my daughter was three, we took her to Peacock Lane, a neighborhood block in southeast Portland that decorates for

Christmas. Most houses go above and beyond, choosing some sort of theme like *The Nightmare Before Christmas* or *Star Wars*. It's festive and noisy and open only to foot traffic for the month leading up to Christmas.

A root had grown under one of the cement blocks, causing a ridge in the sidewalk. It was imperceptible on the dark and crowded street yet just tall enough to trip a toddler. My daughter fell, even while holding my hand. As soon as I heard her crying, I whisked her into my arms. I checked for skinned knees, but she wasn't hurt, only shaken up. "Oh," I said in a soft, soothing voice, "that must have really scared you." As I held her close, she quickly calmed down.

In less than one minute, parents can teach their children something important about emotions. When she is thrown off-balance, she feels something in her body that expresses itself in tears. A parent can translate that bodily sensation into a feeling she can talk about: "scared." Then parents can teach their kids how to manage that feeling. In this situation my daughter came to me believing I would hold her close and talk in soothing tones until she was able to move on from the emotion. In moments like this, children learn that emotions are for connection. *If I cry, my mom or dad will come and hold me.* This is how children begin to understand what emotions are about and why they are important in relationships.

But imagine what happens to the child who is subtly shamed for her feelings instead of being held. What if her parent's only response to every cry is, "You're fine," without assessing whether she's really been hurt. Or what if her parent ignores her needs? And what if this response happened over and over again, teaching her that emotions either have no value or, worse, they cause rejection and disconnection. What if she learns that crying only makes Dad angry? Then emotions do the opposite of drawing others close—she learns that they cause disconnection.

If early on in life you found that showing emotions like sadness or worry didn't draw others close, it only makes sense to lock your emotions in the basement. Instead, if you were subtly or explicitly punished for sharing distressing emotions, you quickly learned not to show them at all or, if possible, not to feel them in the first place.

So refusing to share your emotions isn't a way of icing others out; it's a way of keeping them close. Over the course of a lifetime, locking away emotions becomes an automatic response, occurring outside of consciousness. Many of my clients so deftly lock away emotion that they have trouble interrupting the process when their spouse asks, "But what are you feeling?" The feeling has already gone to the basement, untouched and inaccessible.

Psychological Insight

Someone who automatically shuts down their emotions creates a biological pattern in their brain that dismisses input from the insula, the part of the brain that helps us interpret bodily sensations as emotions, as well as read the body language of others.[2] Over time, accessing their emotions, as well as reading those of others, becomes increasingly difficult. Their brain has shifted to help them avoid emotions.

EMOTIONAL FIRE HAZARDS

After spending so much time and energy suppressing your own emotions, it can be frustrating when others don't do the same. This frustration is like taking great care to be safe on the Fourth of July, and then all your neighbors shoot off fireworks that inevitably land in the driest part of your lawn. To avoid any fires, you not only hose down your own space, but you also try to extinguish everyone else's yards.

Because others probably don't appreciate your cold, wet spray to their emotions, you prefer to be alone, putting up high walls to make sure that stray fireworks don't set your yard on fire. It becomes so much easier to be alone because there's less to manage, so you retreat into patterns that give you solitude and a feeling of safety, protected from the world of emotions that others might bring in.

Inevitably, connecting with others becomes hard. Someone important in your life tells you about their feelings and expects the same from you. You reach inside and find nothing, not knowing it's all locked in the basement. Realizing you have nothing to show, you feel like you let the other person down. Over time, you develop performance anxiety when it comes to emotions. As one client told me, "It's like being on stage, holding my instrument, and the rest of the band starts to play. And then I suddenly realize I've never practiced a day in my life." You have no idea how to connect emotionally.

So you avoid going on stage. You avoid deep conversation, intimate moments, and any possibility of meaningful talk. You want to do activities with others because you *do* want connection, but you can't risk getting too personal. So you build things together or play board games or do outdoor activities.

But what happens when you shut down your emotions with God?

SHUTDOWN ATTACHMENT STYLE IN SPIRITUALITY

Perhaps the biggest reason you keep your emotions locked in the basement is because you have been told you shouldn't have them in the first place. You aren't fazed when you hear that your worry or sadness offends God, because that response is no different from that of other important people in your life. You expect that sharing your worry or sorrow or doubt will only cause more disappointment. So faith becomes an effective tool to lock away your unseemly emotions, hoping no one sees them. The practices of a shutdown attachment style can show up in different ways, but they all have the same goal: to shut down uncomfortable emotions, to manage your own internal world, and to make sure that you're not too anxious or sad or doubtful for God to want to be close to you.

There are books upon books that offer concrete answers to questions of faith. How do we know we're saved? What will the end times be like? What's God's design for family, governments, and faith communities? How do you tell whether you are within the faith or outside the bounds of it? Is our eternal fate predetermined, or do we have free will? When, how, and why did God create the universe? Who will be judged by God and who won't? Why did miracles happen, and do they still happen? What are angels and demons? What exactly did Jesus's death mean to accomplish—and how? How can we identify what is the Holy Spirit and what's our own self-deception? How do justification and sanctification work? What's the role of baptism? Does something special happen when we take the bread and the wine? Does it have to be wine?

The life of faith encourages these questions because you want to connect with a mysterious God. But take it from someone who reads a lot of books on theology: sometimes it's easier to trust a system of beliefs than a living God who personally engages with us. With a shutdown attachment style, you try to contain the truth of God in a set of doctrinal statements because if we can figure out the left-brained mechanics of it all, we can avoid uncomfortable emotions. But connection with God requires engaging beyond a scientific approach to theology. We end up trusting a dogma, not a Divine Parent.

In shutdown spirituality, theological systems become the oven mitts with which to hold the red-hot threat of human experience, full of emotions and heartache, in an attempt to avoid being burned. We believe that if we learn enough information, emotions can be vanquished and conquered. So we search for some type of dogma in a hope that it will solve the swirling sea of feelings we struggle with, seeking out a concrete way of making sense of life. Some seek theological truths, others bank on political ideologies that help us create meaning of the struggles we experience and see in the world. We focus on the way things "should be" and learn a practical system of rules for getting there. To suppress our uncomfortable emotions, shutdown attachment disengages the heart and takes shelter in the head.

Pádraig Ó Tuama wrote about a church poster he once saw that advertised faith, hope, and *certainty* (a slightly different take on Paul's teaching on faith, hope, and *love*). We think if we hold all the answers, we can calm down. Many approach the Bible this way, as a book of facts and rules that, if followed closely, will prevent pain. If we follow biblical principles for financial stewardship, we won't have to experience the stress of economic hardships. If we raise our kids God's way, then we won't have to face the pain of children who rebel. If we remember the promise of resurrection, we won't have to grieve like those who have no hope—which has often been taken to mean we don't grieve at all. If the Bible explains the cause and effect of everything, then we have a way to grasp a sense of control and understanding that will rescue us from the tumultuous experience of being human in a broken world. This approach to faith shuts down the uncomfortable experience of being human, including all its difficult questions and the inevitable emotions that flow from them.

SPIRITUAL BYPASS

Spiritual bypass is what happens when we avoid dealing with difficult emotions, trauma, or other challenging parts of life. Instead, we rely on spiritual concepts or platitudes such as "God won't give you more than you can handle" and "When God closes a door, he opens a window." It's not only clichés that are used; standalone Bible verses also fit the bill. During hard times we shove down our anxiety by reminding ourselves that "God works for the good of those who love him,"[3] trusting that everything will turn out fine. All the while, we try to forget that the man who penned those words, the apostle Paul, was repeatedly beaten, imprisoned, stoned, and eventually executed.

If our attachment style always tells us, "You shouldn't feel scared or sad or angry," it makes sense that we would end up enlisting our faith in that goal. So we use our religious tradition as a padlock on the basement door. Sadly, the church has often helped us to that end; in many churches, feelings are demonized as the enemy of truth. For many years, Jeremiah's statement "the heart is deceitful above all things"[4] has been taken to be about our emotions, that we can't trust them, therefore we should ignore them. Men's ministries have run full speed ahead with military metaphors that thrive on extinguishing feelings in favor of the "facts" of faith. These provide biblical license to do what feels natural in the first place: shut yourself off from emotions.

You might feel worried about your kid as she grows into a teenager, but instead of reaching out to a friend for support, you tell yourself, "God's in control, so it will be fine," and send the worry to the basement. A friend doesn't show up to your party, and instead of sharing your hurt feelings, you remind yourself, "The Bible says to forgive," and you try to put the pain out of mind. Or you experience the crushing disappointment of being denied a promotion at work and say, "God's got a better plan for me." Negative feelings about self are ignored in favor of statements of *who I am in Christ*. It seems that as long as you remind yourself of biblical truths, you don't have to experience painful emotions. Of course, there is hope for your pain in healthy spirituality, but shutdown spirituality sidesteps the pain rather than allowing God to meet you in it. You think you can keep these uncomfortable feelings in the basement. This seems to be the only way to make sense of the promise of peace and joy that Jesus offers.

Clint tried to manage his anxiety through a list of biblical truths. He memorized passages like Philippians 4:6: "Do not be anxious about anything, but in every situation, by prayer and petition, with thanksgiving, present your requests to God" and 1 Peter 5:7: "Cast all your anxiety on him because he cares for you."

"So when do you turn to these verses?" I asked him. "What is it that you feel anxious about? What are your cares?"

"I just repeat them in the morning. It helps me keep my head in a good place," he said with a smile that showed genuine pride in his spiritual practices. I told him I was glad that it was so helpful to meditate on these verses.

I paused and then asked in a soft voice, "Do you tell God about these anxieties?" His smile faded slightly, like there was a tiny crack in the veneer. A flash of sadness showed through, and in that moment, I could see the overwhelming worry he carried inside. He'd been trying to use these Bible verses to push these uncomfortable feelings away—a strategy that ultimately didn't work well, which was what had brought him into my office. Rather than engaging with God about his worries, he used God's Word to pretend they didn't exist.

Over the following months, we explored how Clint related to God and assumptions he had about how God saw his feelings— that God expected him not to ever worry because Clint had all the reassurance he needed in the Bible. But eventually, rather than using Bible verses to suppress his worry, Clint allowed God to be *with him in his worry*. It would be long after our work ended that I read Psalm 91:15, in which God says, "He will call on me, and I will answer him; I will be with him in trouble." It's not a promise that we will never be distressed but that God will be with us in our distress, which might feel risky if you've always found that sharing your sadness or worry only drives others away.

If we can live on biblical truth alone, we don't need to let others close—including God. We can "stand alone on the Word of God,"[5] as the children's song goes. It allows us to keep others at arm's length, under the guise of spiritual maturity. We may minister to others, but we'll avoid putting ourselves in situations where we are required to be vulnerable. Our religious framework allows us to avoid our emotions, which keeps us from identifying them within ourselves and sharing them with others. It's a comfortable place to live if your blueprint for relationships tells you that emotions only drive others away.

SPIRITUAL WORKAHOLICS

Just as the four-year-old explores the playground to distract himself from the storm of emotions inside, if you have a shutdown attachment style, you'll look for something to *do* to take you out of your emotions. At the beginning, God gave humans the tasks of naming animals and keeping the garden and also walked with them in the cool of the evening. A shutdown spiritual style latches on to the tasks *for* God to the exclusion of communion *with* God.

Avoiding your emotions is simple enough, so long as you never slow down. You might volunteer for church lawn maintenance or organize the potluck. Or you could run PowerPoint or quietly set up and tear down special events, hanging out in the shadows. It doesn't mean your works of service are duplicitous. You offer your best. Not knowing how to express love in other ways, you search for something concrete to show your love for God and your community. You struggle to find the right words to talk about your affection for God or others, but you know how to show it through acts of love.

Of course, not all volunteers have a shutdown attachment style, but frequent volunteering does offer effective cover if you do. It's a way of staying close to God, just not too close. Certainly, God has given us roles according to our giftings, but shutdown attachment places your whole identity into your responsibilities. Over time God becomes a cosmic boss with an impending deadline. It's all caring for the garden and no walking in the cool of the evening.

Busy distraction doesn't have to be limited to the church either. You might find purpose in work—as you should—and apply your energy to your career or a cause or organization you deeply believe in. You find refuge from your feelings through effort, something that gives meaning to your life and allows you to focus on the external, distracting you from your inner life.

DIFFICULT QUESTIONS

Over time the absence of emotion starts to impact the way we practice our faith. Research indicates that those who reflexively shut down their emotions are much less likely to change their way of thinking when presented with a new perspective.

When you lock away feelings in the basement, you are much less likely to be open to new ways of seeing the world.

That's because information doesn't change your beliefs, experience does.

To see something in a new way, you have to engage emotionally with your own experience and your own memories, harvesting and reorganizing them for a new way of seeing. But if you are always dodging your emotions, you will avoid your own experience, as well as avoiding the experience of others. If you always ignore your own emotional suffering, you'll likely take the same approach to the suffering of others.

There's always risk when stepping into someone else's shoes: we might feel a little bit of what they are feeling, which also touches on a little bit of what we are feeling. As Brené Brown says, "Empathy is a vulnerable choice because in order to connect with you, I have to connect with something within myself that knows that feeling."[6]

Research Insight

Research shows that those with a shutdown attachment style are much less likely to change their beliefs about a particular issue, because often changing the way we view a particular issue is often linked to an emotional experience that causes us to reevaluate our beliefs.[7] A common example would be that many white people have changed their belief about the prevalence of racism in US society only after hearing the personal stories of people who have experienced it.

All this sounds unbearable to those of us who manage emotions by pushing them away. In our reluctance to manage our feelings, we cling to cold, hard facts when we hear stories that might spark some emotion in us. It feels safer *not* to step into the shoes of another person if doing so means that the anxiety-squashing beliefs we have clung to are brought into question.

If we've dealt with suffering we see in the world by coming up with cause-and-effect systems of theology, then we will cling to those systems to avoid the more difficult questions. For instance, we may think those experiencing heartbreaking poverty are simply experiencing the consequences of their actions. When we believe everyone's quality of life is the result *only* of their own choices, it's easier to turn a blind eye to suffering.

We've quelled our anxiety by having all the right answers, so we have to hold a rigid way of approaching the world and our faith. The moment our "right answers" come under scrutiny, our anxiety rises—and then often anger comes. Maybe you've been a part of a religious community like this, where asking questions is experienced as a threat, evoking fear and anxiety followed by anger and suppression.

SHUTTING DOWN EMOTIONS MEANS SHUTTING DOWN CLOSENESS

If we lock our emotions in the basement in an attempt to keep God close, something else happens: we end up feeling distant. Intimacy happens in the emotional interactions of a relationship, and when we hide our emotions from God, we never get the closeness we long for. Bonding is built on responsiveness, feeling that others understand our emotional experiences and that they care. It's how we know we matter to others. But if we don't ever share our emotions with God, true bonding never happens.

Suppressing our emotions also cripples our ability to engage in true community with others. When we can't share our emotions, or respond to the emotions of others, we never experience the belonging we were built for. We might feel like teammates or coworkers but never the family that the apostle Paul describes in his letters to the church. We show up with our bodies but have trouble connecting heart-to-heart. Our life of faith ends up feeling lonely.

THE CORE OF SHUTDOWN ATTACHMENT

"I'm sorry I'm crying."

Garrett looked down, barely choking out the words. I could see his hands were trembling slightly as the tears splashed onto his palms. Although he was in his midtwenties, he'd inherited the stoicism of his father's generation, which was then cemented in the culture of rural community that had descended from German immigrant farmers who had barely survived the Great Depression. I could almost feel the visceral shame in his body that came from shedding tears in front of another person.

I'd asked him about what it was like when his boss told him earlier in the week that he wasn't cutting it at work, even though I could tell he'd feel more comfortable talking about anything else. He eventually told me he felt like a failure, and that was when the tears started.

Garrett wasn't the first person who has apologized for crying in my office. But Garrett was different. He made a sound of disgust. "I hate this," he said quietly. I could tell there was a tornado of negative self-talk inside about not being strong enough to keep from crying.

"That makes so much sense to me," I responded, "that showing your emotions like this would feel *so* uncomfortable. I'm sure no one in your life has seen this, seen you crying—and been okay with it, anyway. But I'm so glad to see this part of you. I've known about your sadness for a long time, and to see it like this, in your tears, makes me feel more connected. It makes me like you more, actually." He was quiet.

I continued, "I know how hard you try all the time. It's got to be exhausting. And then when you fail, it's like it's all for nothing."

He nodded, still unable to talk.

"I wonder if you could ever tell your wife about this, what it's like to try so hard at work and feel like such a failure." I said softly, "I know *I* like hearing about it. And from what you've told me, this is the sort of thing she says she wants to hear about."

He shook his head, and more tears came.

I told him it was okay to cry, okay to be quiet, and that I was honored he let me see his sadness. "This is hard work. You've done such hard work today," I said.

This was the start of Garrett's healing. It would be months before his body relaxed a little when he shared his worry or sadness with me and many months later that he eventually shared some of these feelings with his wife. Eventually, he found that—unlike in the family he grew up in—showing sadness or worry brought people close. He found that not only could his wife handle these vulnerable emotions, she *wanted* to hear about them. And he found that sharing them led to deeper connection.

A GOD WHO CAN HANDLE OUR TEARS

Jen Wilkin writes, "We must love God with our minds, allowing our intellect to inform our emotions, rather than the other way around."[8] But if we only love God with our minds, we miss out on the spontaneity of authentic, intimate relationship with God that we see throughout the Psalms and the rest of Scripture. When we listen to our hearts and share our feelings with God, we find connection with a Divine Parent who longs to hear our emotions and help us understand them.

When we love God with our vulnerable hearts, we find that he understands that Bible verses don't always take away the painful parts of life and who knows that doubt and anxiety and sadness are all part of life in a broken world. This is the kind of God who weeps when Lazarus dies, even though he knows about resurrection. A God who can handle our anger when the world is unfair. One who can hear that sometimes it doesn't seem like "in all things God works for the good of those who love him."[9] We need God to understand that emotions can overwhelm us and we're not even sure how to access them. We need a parent who will help us make sense of our emotions, rather than shame us for having them in the first place.

King David talks about this kind of Divine Parent. In Psalm 139:1, he writes, "You have searched me, LORD, and you know me." David doesn't show any anxiety that what's in his basement will scare God away. Even though he asks God to find "any offensive way"[10] in him, it's clear that he believes nothing will drive God away. He knows that anywhere he goes, "your hand will guide me, your right hand will hold me fast."[11]

David's emotions are woven throughout his spiritual life; it's part of why he was known as a man after God's heart. He tells God about his joy, his gratitude, his sadness, his anxiety, his doubt, his guilt, his grief. He brings it all to the table, expecting that God can handle it—and will respond. This is what we truly need. We need a God who doesn't want only our best but wants all of us.

We see this same God, who sees our innermost being and accepts us, in the Gospels. Having emotions locked in the basement reminds me of when the disciples hid behind locked doors. In the wake of Jesus's death, they were terrified and locked away in a dark room, not unlike what we do with our own fear in shutdown spirituality. Yet Jesus shows up in the dark and says, "Peace be with you!"[12] He breaks into the scary parts of human experience, and rather than being offended, he simply greets us, delighted to be with us—even in the locked-up rooms within us.

BREAKING INTO THE BASEMENT

After a lifetime of automatically sending emotions to the basement, finding out what you're feeling can be difficult. If you have a shutdown attachment style, my goal is not to make you someone you're not. You don't have to be the most emotional person in the room; the goal is balance. We want facts *and* feelings. But the second part can be incredibly hard.

If you've grown up in a home or faith tradition that forces

you to choose between emotions and relationship, even dipping a toe in the world of feelings is scary. Your body will remember on a visceral level and try to hide them away. When you're told not to feel certain emotions by those you love most, you often do so with vigor. Changing that pattern is difficult but not impossible. In fact, I find that those with a shutdown style just need to be shown the ropes, and then they find that identifying and sharing emotions was a natural ability within them all along.

Many clients I work with know they are supposed to "sit with their feelings" but have no idea how. Let's break it down into concrete steps. Most emotions originate in the body as sensations—a tension in the chest or clenching of your gut. Those signals move up into your brain stem to be interpreted by your brain. The goal of this exercise is not to figure out your emotions but simply to take the small step of noticing the sensations in your body.

Brief Body Scan Exercise

1. Sit upright in a comfortable position. Take three intentional breaths. They don't have to be deep breaths, just comfortable and grounding.
2. Notice your whole body, and see if you notice any immediate sensations. It might be pain in your neck, hunger in your stomach, or a little tension in your chest. Or maybe you feel numbness. You might notice a heaviness in your shoulders. Don't jump to interpreting the sensation; just notice it.
3. If paying attention to your whole body feels overwhelming, start with your toes, and move up along your legs, noticing each part until you reach your head.

4. Rather than judging these sensations, try to notice them simply as data.

5. That's it. Great job. If you make a habit of noticing your body sensations twice a day, it's a great foundation for knowing and engaging with your emotions.

IMMANUEL IN THE BASEMENT

You're not a cold-hearted monster if you have a shutdown attachment style. It's just that early on you were forced to choose between relationship and emotion. If those you loved most saw what you were feeling, they would turn their backs and run—that's what it felt like, anyway. But a shutdown spirituality doesn't fit with a God who created us for relationship, since emotions are what relationships are made of. Through sharing our emotions, we connect with one another, creating a sense of closeness. It is how we experience Immanuel, God with us.

To share your emotions with God, you first need to know, on a gut level, that God can handle them. You need to know that your sadness or worry will be seen not as a lack of faith that drives God away but as a cry for comfort that will bring nearness. God shows up in your locked basement and says, "Peace be with you," as Jesus did with the disciples. Please know that in the middle of your fear and chaos, God is with you and wants to hear your emotions—even the bad ones.

Chapter Five

SHAME-FILLED SPIRITUALITY

"Me and the Big Guy have an agreement," Lenny says with a pained smile, "I don't like him, and he don't like me."

"Which came first?" I ask, meeting his eyes with a smirk, matching his dark whimsy.

"Well," he says, leaning back with a groan, back sore from a lifetime of masonry work in the cold upper Midwest, before continuing, "seems like he's had it out for me for a long time."

A year ago, when Lenny first came to see me, he spent most of the first session razzing me for a hole that had worn through my dress shoes. I wanted to know his history, how he was feeling, what symptoms he had. He just wanted to talk about the hole in my shoe. Then, of course, my shoe was the first thing he brought up at our second session. He told me that it made him like me. My lack of polish earned me some points in his book. A life full of hard times had made it difficult for him to trust anyone, much less a green therapist like me, nearly half his age, looking like I hadn't done a hard day's work in my whole life. But over our time together, we built trust that showed up in little ways, and he told me that it started with the hole in my shoe.

To be honest, my main strategy with Lenny was to say as little as possible. I was still an intern working toward my counseling license for the state of Minnesota, so I knew any advice I could give would fall flat against the decades of life that he brought into the office. I offered a listening ear, and that seemed to be enough. This particular day, I was asking if he had any form of spirituality that he used to make it through the storms of life, as my clinical training had taught me. But for Lenny, a God in control was a God to blame, so the whole concept offered no comfort in a life of troubles. God clearly did not like him, and in return, he didn't like God.

Lenny isn't alone. Even in the church, many of us believe that although God loves us unconditionally, our Divine Parent doesn't like us all that much. Dr. Nicholas Gibson tells a story of a pastor who asked his congregation to raise their hands if they believed God loved them.[1] Every hand was raised. Then he asked for a raise of hands for those who felt God liked them. All but two or three hands dropped. We might want to come close to God, but we feel we'll be met with Divine displeasure.

Many of us deal with not feeling liked by God in different ways. Lenny protected himself through telling a story that he didn't like God any more than God liked him. But it was only a way of hiding his longing for closeness.

JUDGMENT AND DISAPPOINTMENT

With a shame-filled attachment style, getting close to God comes with a cost: you have to feel terrible about yourself.

Getting close requires us to come face-to-face with a God who always wishes we were more holy, who is always judging us and disappointed with us. At best, the God of shame-filled attachment does not like us, and at worst is utterly disgusted with us. We approach, hoping we will find mercy in spite of how repulsive we are. As R. C. Sproul often said, "We are not sinners because we sin. We sin because we are sinners."[2] So sin is not only something we do, it's the core of who we are—and since we know God hates sin, it's hard to believe that he doesn't also hate us.

In this attachment style, a deep sense of shame thrives. We believe, deep in our gut, that we aren't truly accepted because we have too many flaws. We can never relax into the arms of a God who constantly judges us according to a perfect standard. But at least we can try to get as close as possible by repeatedly demonstrating that we're aware we don't deserve closeness.

SHAME-FILLED FAMILY
RELATIONSHIPS

First let's look at what this dynamic looks like in a family. One of the worst parts about harsh parents is the confusion it creates in a child. The child wants to be close to her parents because, biologically, she is designed to go to them for safety and security. But a part of the child knows there's a risk of criticism, judgment, or even violence. This is the plight of children who are abused, whether emotionally or physically. Their longing for closeness comes into direct conflict with their drive to stay safe. They can stay at a distance and feel lonely or get close and risk being judged or criticized or hurt. The child finds herself in a tornado of conflicting emotions. There's no true solution, just a choice between two bad options.

Brandon desperately wanted closeness with his mom when he was a child, but he knew that getting close to her included the risk of harsh criticism or rejection. Sometimes he could get the hug he wanted, but many times he received the opposite. Some days he could talk with Mom and everything was okay. But on the wrong day, Mom would explode with vitriol: "Why isn't your room clean? You're such a slob!" or "No wonder the neighborhood kids don't want to play with you. You're so annoying!"

Psychological Insight

Researchers have described this attachment style "fright without solution," because children naturally turn to their parents during times of fear but have no solution when the parent is the source of the fear.[3]

Or think about what it would be like to be Ashley, whose parents never say outright that she's done something wrong. But as soon as she steps a toe out of line, she can feel the walls of isolation that rise up around her. Her dad ices her out, brimming with silent rage. Her mom gets quiet too, and it's like the whole world has stopped and she's left all alone in a terrifying place.

In a split second, she finds herself stuck in a still-face moment for hours, and the silence says, *I wish you weren't here* or, worse, *I wish you weren't my child*. In actuality, her dad might not be thinking those things, but the message comes across loud and clear to a child.

Let's consider a more extreme but unfortunately common scenario. How does a child get close to a parent who is nurturing and loving one day but drunk and violent the next? Regardless of what the parent may say, the physical harm says, *I despise you*. Beyond the physical pain lies the excruciating feeling of being unwanted and disliked by the person who is supposed to delight in you and hold you close.

Then there are children who never get the closeness they yearn for. There's no abuse, just a soul-crushing absence of attention or care or comfort. Ben grew up in a family where everyone seemed happy enough, yet at the same time, it felt like no one knew him at all. No one asked what his day was like or had the time to understand his world. He felt starved of his parents' attention, and the absence of connection communicated clearly: *you're nothing but an inconvenience; you're not worthy of connection or belonging.*[4]

Childhood Abuse

If these family dynamics seem familiar, https://www.childwelfare.gov has definitions of childhood abuse for clarification. If these parent-child dynamics were present in your home growing up, contacting a local licensed mental health provider may provide clarity and steps forward in healing.

All these interactions communicate a common message: *I don't want to be close to you because there is something wrong with you.* The child is then caught in a catch-22. They can either isolate themselves to feel safe yet desperately lonely, or they can seek the closeness they desire despite the risk of receiving the painful message that they are broken and repulsive.

ALL ROTTEN INSIDE

These experiences create a sense that something is wrong with you, a deep sense of shame. Dr. Karyn Purvis spent her life working with children who experienced the worst types of disconnection that the world can offer, dedicating her work to children "from hard places," a term she coined for those in foster care or those who had experienced other forms of attachment trauma. She found that children often talked about feeling rotten inside, a sense that something at their core is vile and disgusting. Other psychologists have talked about the feeling that "there's something clearly and palpably bad about self, something that deserves judgment or disgust."[5] Attachment textbooks are full of vivid descriptions of this terrible feeling: "a sense of deformity, degradation, or worthlessness . . . ugliness and undesirability," or feeling "revolting and untouchable . . . unfit to live among other human beings."[6]

The worst part of shame is that it provides continual felt evidence that there's something broken within you that drives others away. It makes you feel disgusting, as if you can't get close to others until the shame is gone—until you're "fixed." Maybe you lost hope of being fixed long ago. It's as if you'll never be good enough to be close with the ones you love.

Because this shame is both subtle and ever-present, it's tough to recognize. As I work with clients to put a name to this feeling, they often tell me they simply knew it as *normal life*. Like oxygen, it'd been there as long as they could remember, such a constant fixture throughout the years that it was hardly worth mentioning. One client told me, "It's like there's this black ink I have to hold inside that will spill out onto anyone who gets close." Shame has become such a part of your self-concept that there are moments it's hard to look inside and see anything but a disgusting goo. Though hard to put a finger on, shame drives your relational worlds in drastic and enduring ways.

Intimacy is incredibly difficult because of the fear that others will see what's inside you and be disgusted. Shame puts you in a position of longing for closeness but also fearing it at the same time.

You go through life condemning yourself for being so selfish or annoying or dishonest or whatever it is that makes you unworthy of love. You then grow into an adult, believing that these aspects of your personality make you unfit for relationships. If only you could change, maybe just a little more, *then* you could get the closeness you need. After all, that's the message you've gotten from your parents: *there's something wrong with you, and if you could be a little less like yourself, I would like you more.* You hate the parts of yourself that keep you from love, precisely *because* you want so badly to be loved. If you punish yourself enough, you might just be transformed into someone others could fully embrace.

Even when it's not a conscious thought, your body language communicates that you know you are unlovable. Your self-isolation shows through slouching your shoulders, looking at the floor, and avoiding eye-contact. You don't expect closeness, and your body shows that you believe you don't deserve embrace. And when others do come close, you become nervous that they'll see that there's something wrong with you.

NEVER GOOD ENOUGH

Not unlike abused children, some of us have been told that there's something at our core that drives God away, which mirrors the description that emotional abuse survivors feel: "something clearly and palpably bad about self, something that deserves judgment or disgust,"[7] to use the words from an attachment-science book.

We're also told that our sinful hearts are disgusting to God, driving separation between us.

When I was growing up, my mom would often quote Max Lucado: "God loves you just the way you are," which was followed by a catch: "but He refuses to leave you that way. He wants you to be just like Jesus."[8] The second part was a stab in my side. God may love me, but I obviously wasn't liked much because I was very far off from looking like Jesus. It was a reminder that God would be so much happier with a better version of myself. A dark cloud of displeasure loomed over the relationship, a constant itch in the back of my mind that God always thought I could be doing better, trying harder. God was not particularly fond of me as I continued to fall far below his perfect standard.

I knew that God was disgusted with my shadowy parts, finding them off-putting, as holiness cannot tolerate the slightest sin. "God actually does demand perfection," wrote author Kristen Wetherell. "There is no exception for grumbling about the weather. There is no loophole for a moment's lustful glance. There is no leeway for failing to worship."[9] God's pleasure is to make us perfect like himself, and he does not grade on a curve. God loves us, but he does not love the ugly parts of us.

Let me be clear, in this framework God is pleased with us *to the extent that we have been transformed from who we once were.* Unfortunately, many of us feel we are still those very people, sullied by our everyday actions. Many of us, myself included, find that we never feel holy enough to get close to God.

When righteousness is how we get close to God and sin is how we become far, we desperately try to eradicate the foul parts of us, hoping to get the closeness we need. But it never works, because we will never live up to the standard of perfection, despite how much we might grow and mature and become people who love others well. Nouwen writes about the common feeling of being the "nakedness to God's intruding eye,"[10] crumbling under the weight of "scrupulosity, guilt-feelings, fear for punishment, unbearable responsibilities and unlivable expectations."[11] We know there is nowhere to hide from the endlessly judgmental eyes of God.

Throughout Scripture, God is always calling us to holiness. But there is a huge difference between a God who expects us to be perfect *before* coming close and a God who comes close to help us grow in maturity and sanctification. If we expect only judgment from God, we will want to keep some distance. If we know that God understands us and wants to help us walk in healthier ways, we can relax and draw close.

My experience as a therapist has helped shift me away from shame-filled spirituality. People often come into my office with behaviors that hurt themselves and others. But I don't tell them to get out of my office until they've become better people. I am so glad to spend time with them and to help them grow and heal. They don't even need to know *how* to grow and change—I can help them with that. I just need them to take some steps of trust with me as we walk forward together. God approaches us in a similar way, wanting to walk through the journey of healing and growth together.

However, many Christian communities have downplayed teachings of a God who wishes to heal us and emphasized a God who only judges us, simmering with resentment and disappointment. We end up feeling alone in our sin, unsure how to change yet knowing we should. Often we feel stuck and unable to become holy enough to get close to God.

SECOND BEST

When we can't seem to be quite holy enough to get close to God, we try to sidle up close in a different way. If we can't eradicate the unholy parts of us, then at least we can hate them. As a consolation prize, we can join with God by hating what God hates, and we presume that's parts of ourselves.

We hope that if we shame ourselves for not being good enough, God will be pleased with our own self-criticism enough to come close to us. Paul Tillich wrote that when we "cannot contribute anything positive"[12] to getting close to God, "then we try at least to contribute something negative—the pain of self-accusation and self-rejection."[13] Since we think God hates the shadowy parts of us, we try to join the effort and "perform an emotional work of self-punishment,"[14] as Tillich calls it. So closeness becomes partnered with feeling terrible. Even so, we are never sure that God really wants to be close.

Psychological Insight

Research shows that we can withstand physical pain so long as we maintain connection with others, but shame is uniquely painful because it is disconnection from others.[15]

Of course, we know we can approach the throne of grace with confidence because of the cross. Yet somehow even the cross doesn't get us the closeness we long for. Unlike Mr. Rogers, who likes us "just the way" we are, a shame-filled attachment style feels like God accepts us *in spite of* who we are, a notion that continually undermines feeling secure with God.

Untangling Evangelicalism

Sinclair Ferguson wrote, "It is misleading to say that God accepts us the way we are. Rather, he accepts us despite the way we are."[16] Teachings like this can give us a picture of a God who begrudgingly welcomes us, rather than a God who runs to embrace us.

I once went to a church where we received communion each week, always preceded by a reminder that we were wretches undeserving of love. Of course, this pastor included himself in the indictment because if we can't be good enough to get closeness, at least we can remind ourselves and God that we know we aren't. Here, at the heart of connection with God, we have to pass through the painful reminder that we are despicable. We can get closeness, but it comes with the catch of feeling shame.

Similarly, children who are severely abused by their parents will still feel bonded to them.

Sarah's mother verbally abuses Sarah and her siblings. But for Sarah, the idea of setting a boundary and telling her mother, "No more," was too big a risk. She knew that her mother might just as likely cut her off, so putting up with the mistreatment seemed better than losing the connection she had with her mother, flawed though it was.

Attachment science shows us that we are willing to go through immense pain to get the closeness we were created for. Unfortunately, this also happens in faith—we stay close to a God who is disgusted with us, just to get the connection we long for.

GOD MIGHT ACTUALLY WANT ME?

Lenny leans in toward me as though telling a secret. "I know where I'm going," he says softly. "I've done a lot of shit in my life, so I *know* where I'm going." He had ingested the free-floating theology that permeates the air of society: good people go to heaven, bad people go to hell. And he knew which category he fit into.

Discussing a client's spiritual beliefs is permissible and often helpful, as long as I keep tabs on how helpful the discussion is to our therapy work. I don't want the person to feel pressured, preached at, or like I'm asking them to take on my beliefs.

"Some traditions," I say tentatively, "like some Eastern Orthodox churches," trying to sound as objective as possible, "say hell is a time where the unloving parts of us are burned away but that God never leaves us." I was not purporting this as truth but informing him about the variety of views in the Christian tradition.

I watch to see how he takes this information. With a quick wit I've never been able to contend with, Lenny has a knack for wise cracks, especially when the situation gets serious. It's a marvelous tool for protecting vulnerable parts of himself without directly shutting me out. By this point in our work together, I've learned it's his way of keeping me at arm's length without entirely pushing me away.

But instead of making a joke, he lets his eyes soften. In a quiet voice, he says, "I don't mind burning for a while as long as God wants to keep me around."

In one quick sentence, his walls of animosity collapse, revealing a deep longing to be loved and accepted. He's even willing to bear the torture of hell if it means there is hope that God might actually want him. Like a child who will come close to a parent who physically harms them, we will seek closeness in spite of pain. We will willingly go through punishment, even at our own hands, if it means a chance at closeness and belonging. We will continually shame ourselves for being imperfect if it means God might stick around.

CHANGE MY HEART, OH GOD

Just as Lenny was willing to go through hell to be with God, we will put ourselves through the hell of self-hatred to maintain connection with God. When we grow into faith with a God who is disgusted with us, it's easy to end up hating ourselves. Like we're using a Magic Eraser on the wall, we scrub away at the stain of sin, but instead we remove the paint underneath it. It becomes nearly imperceptible to tell where the sin starts and where we stop. Theologian Brad Jersak points out the collateral damage of this internal war: "Hatred of sin and self-hatred and hatred of the sinner are a very thin line, aren't they?"[17]

"Change my heart, Oh God," we cry, and what we mean is, "Make me into someone you actually can stand to be around." God would prefer us to be a little less ourselves, a little more like Jesus, before we can truly have the connection we long for. Often it feels like we must be incredibly holy people before even considering approaching God, or else risk the pain of judgment and criticism and disgust.

Mother Teresa hoped to close the distance between her and God, with the goal of ceasing to exist. "I must disappear completely—if I want God to have the whole," she wrote.[18] We've heard this message many places. After noting John the Baptist's statement, "He must increase, but I must decrease,"[19] we think if decreasing a little is good, completely disappearing is better. We try to extinguish our very personhood. If we could just not be our horrible selves, we reason, then we could get the love we deeply desire.

The apostle Paul talks about imitating Christ for good reason.[20] In Jesus we see someone who is grounded in his belovedness and who sees belovedness in all others. Jesus clearly shows us that God is love,[21] and through his life and teachings, we are called as children of God into that same way of love. But in the modern-day church, the idea of being "just like Jesus"[22] has often been taken to mean we should become less like our unique selves, as though there were something inherently wrong with the way God created us. Sometimes it has even meant we are supposed to become "Jesus-robots"[23] that reflect him to the exclusion of reflecting the unique ways we were made in the image of God.

The constant focus on becoming someone better can often leave us hating who we are now. We think we might be lovable in the future, while feeling intense shame for who we are currently. We wait for the day we will be changed, "in the twinkling of an eye,"[24] into someone more lovable. But until then, we resign ourselves to falling short of feeling that we truly belong.

There are reasons to change and grow and heal and transform, but getting closer to God is not one of them. If we try to change ourselves because we fear disconnection, it won't lead to healing. If we conclude that we are the problem, then we think the solution is to get rid of ourselves, often through self-destructive ways. Martin Luther flagellated himself, ate dirt, and slept in a cell without a blanket in an effort to be holier. He stated in his Ninety-Five Theses that "inner repentance is worthless unless it produces various outward mortification of the flesh."[25]

In current times, shame-filled attachment can look like fasting or committing yourself to spiritual practices *from a place of self-punishment*, hoping it forms you into someone that God will like more. Or it could be constantly berating yourself with self-critical thoughts. Or continually confessing to God that you know how horrible you are. If we can hate who we are, it might motivate us to change into someone who would be good enough to get close to God.

FEELING LESS SECURE

Danielle Shroyer wrote, "For some, the extreme distance between themselves and God is so great, they have to use damaging language to describe themselves,"[26] making statements like, "I'm worthless to God, I'm nothing but a pile of rags, I'm a worm." But, she writes, "there is nothing of God in such an act. That's not faithful, but harmful."[27] This pattern of talking about ourselves reinforces our feelings of shame.

The more that we tell ourselves and God that we don't deserve love, the harder it becomes to believe we are loved. While praising God for unending love, we quickly slip into shame-filled spirituality: "You love me even though there's nothing lovable about me," or "I'm such a wretch. I can't believe you would love someone like me."

Each time we make these types of statements, it's another reinforcement that we are fundamentally broken in a way that disqualifies us from love, and this belief has harmful consequences. "Self-rejection is the greatest enemy of spiritual life," wrote Henri Nouwen, "because it contradicts the sacred voice that calls us the 'Beloved.'"[28] Surely God's love is brighter than our darkness, but constant self-denigration doesn't help us increase our security with God. It works as a fertilizer for shame to grow.

Untangling Evangelicalism

"Adam and Eve deserved the ultimate silent treatment for all eternity," writes Matt Smethurst.[29] What a painful thing it is to believe we deserve eternal disconnection.

Returning to Brené Brown's definition of shame as "the intensely painful feeling or experience of believing that we are flawed and therefore unworthy of love and belonging,"[30] we can see how we tell this shame narrative in churches, often about ourselves: "God loves me even though he has no reason to." It's as though God made a mistake in loving us. We call ourselves "the scum of the earth"[31] without recognizing that when Paul used this phrase, he was referring to the way the world saw the first apostles, not the way God saw them.

Constant reiterations of our unworthiness reinforce the worst parts of a shame-filled attachment style. It confirms that we deserve to be rejected, a visceral and painful feeling. It tells us that as we get close to God, we should brace ourselves for judgment and rejection. The more we shame ourselves in an attempt to tell about God's mercy, the more we weave our feelings of worthlessness into our spirituality.

Somehow, along the way, we've lost the story of a Parent who wraps us in a huge hug, embracing the whole of us, pig slop and all. We need a secure base, even when we've blown it all, a Parent who meets us with great delight just to be near us, absent of resentment or stifled frustration or disgust. This is a Parent who understands what connection is all about and knows what we need to feel safe and secure in a relationship.

Rather than a God who loves us in spite of who we are, we need a God who delights in who we are, in spite of what we've done.

Underneath all the shame, we want to know we are liked just as we are. Because we want to be accepted, we try to hate the parts of ourselves that would make us unacceptable. When we find ourselves embracing a shame-filled attachment style, it helps to understand what our needs are: to be accepted and to be loved. Not unlike children, we simply want to be loved.

OBSCURING THE *IMAGO DEI*

When we speak about ourselves as deserving only punishment, it gives us license to treat others the same. Unfortunately, when we believe that humans are unworthy of love, we lose sight of the *imago Dei* in every person. The belief that we are destined for punishment allows the violence and death embedded in our systems to go unchallenged, and sometimes baptized as though God-ordained. Mako Nagasawa believes that one of the main influences on high rates of incarceration in the US is the Christian church's overemphasis on God's role as a divine punisher.[32] He's argued that because we've believed God is more likely to punish sinners than heal them into wholeness, we have treated offenders in our society in similar ways.

Theological Insight

The idea of what we deserve is a philosophical question. If God chooses mercy rather than punishment, by what standard can we argue that we deserve punishment? This leads us into deep theological conversations, asking if God is bound by certain laws or if God's actions determine the laws. (Does God *have to* punish sinners *because* he is holy? Or does God get to decide?) The current idea that God must punish is partly the by-product of medieval theologian Anselm of Canterbury making the gospel relevant in the eleventh century. He used the metaphor of a serf offending the honor of a royalty, unable to restore honor because of the serf's ignoble status. It was based in a feudal culture that has long since passed in the millennium since it was written.

A few years ago, in the wake of another death of a black man at the hands of the police, I saw multiple examples of a shame-filled approach to God. When police officers killed Eric Garner, I saw Christians reasoning that because everyone has sinned and offended a holy God, execution is what everyone deserves—and in fact that was what Eric Garner deserved. In that moment, shame-filled spirituality was upholding an unjust system that had no vision for the inherent value of humans, whom God created. We need freedom from shame-filled spirituality not only to escape our own shame but also to heal our systems that use shame to oppress and abuse.

BEING BELOVED

Stepping into secure spirituality means experiencing the truth that God doesn't just bear with us—God delights in us as beloved children. Attachment research has shown that delight is one of the keys to a secure attachment. It makes sense because being liked creates emotional safety where we can relax rather than perform. Our bodies respond to being in the presence of someone who likes us: our shoulders will fall slightly, and our nervous system can move into a more relaxed state. Theologian James Alison said that being liked by God is "a power so gentle and so huge."[33]

"Being the Beloved expresses the core truth of our existence," wrote Nouwen.[34] We all know God loves us, but God's delight is a whole other matter. We need a God who looks beneath our sin and shame and sees a beloved child. A relational God created us for a relationship in holy communion. True connection happens when we are delighted in, brought close not *in spite* of who we are but because of who we are. Danielle Shroyer puts it plainly: "Who we are, before anyone else, is children of God."[35] There is no greater truth about who we are as God's creation.

Based on the popular teaching that God can't stand sin, we'd expect that God would be disgusted with humans, especially those least holy in society. Surprisingly, when Jesus comes to earth, he doesn't start puking everywhere. He's not disgusted. He delights in people, loves spending time and sitting at tables with those who would never have been welcomed into the temple. Jesus, the perfect picture of God, delights in us.

This doesn't mean God's not upset about harmful systems in the world—Jesus culled corruption from the temple by overturning tables. But clearly he delights in people, including those marginalized by oppressive religious structures. When he drove out the money changers, he was interrupting a system that harmed the everyday Jews who were being crushed under the weight of an exploitative religious system. Even his wrath was driven by compassion and care for those who were suffering.

I grew up being told that I might look good on the outside, but underneath it all, I'm bad—and fit for eternal disconnection. But the opposite is true. We might behave in all sorts of unhealthy ways, suffering with our bodies of death, but beneath it all, we are loved and created by a God who delights in us.

Delight is the dance we see between parents and children who are loved well. Parents are so happy to see their children, not because of anything they've done or any benefit of what they bring but simply for who they are. My eyes light up when I see my kids after a night away, or I melt when they mispronounce words. My delight isn't based on anything other than our relationship. I simply adore them because of who they are, and our Divine Parent is no different.

HOPE FOR SHAME-FILLED ATTACHMENT

Believing that God delights in us is not always easy because this story about our unlovability resides in the experiential part of our brains. That means we can't change it through new information alone. As my friend K.J. Ramsey wrote in her book, *This Too Shall Last*, "The chasm between who God says he is and who we experience him to be is not crossed by whipping our minds into submission with more theological facts."[36] We need the experience of being accepted and loved before we can change the story.

For some of us who have been discipled into a shame-filled attachment style, it's hard to imagine that God looks at us with anything other than judgment or contempt. Sometimes we need a different experience to help us understand God's love. So try this exercise.

The Loving Face of God

1. Think of someone who likes you. It could be a partner, a family member, a good friend, a mentor—or even a pet.
2. Close your eyes, and imagine their face. What does it look like when you first greet them? Imagine the shape of their eyes, the upturn of their smile.
3. Notice how your body feels as you focus. Your shoulders might relax, or you might feel your gut stop clenching.
4. Now, without putting pressure on yourself, gently consider that perhaps this is a better picture of God's feeling toward you than what you've been told.
5. How does this new picture compare with your usual picture of God?
6. If God delighted in you in this way, how might this change your style of relating to God?

LOOKING FOR GOOD NEWS

Whether you have a more anxious, shutdown, or shame-filled attachment style, you probably have times when it feels incredibly hard to trust that God loves you and wants to be near you.

You try to connect with God, but that pursuit of connection can be exhausting or even excruciating. You long for a God who wants to connect even more than you do, whose presence brings you into refuge, rest, and comfort.

You've been given the "good news," and yet you struggle to feel consistently close to God. You don't need just good news—you need better news! Let's return to the story of Scripture—the record of God's interactions with us that I expect you're well familiar with—to find some better news that not only provides a more solid theological framework to hold in your mind but also inspires better spiritual practices that bring good news into your heart and body.

Chapter Six

A CLEARER PICTURE

Jesus came to set the record straight about what God is like.

He spent much of his ministry talking about what God and the kingdom are like. He tried to show us the truth about what God is like because, back then and now, distorted pictures of God creep in everywhere, even among those who aim to tell "a simple message . . . that comes straight from God's Word,"[1] such as world-renowned evangelist Billy Graham.

Billy Graham, perhaps one of the most well-known Christians in modern times, told his own parable about what God is like. In a sermon, Graham said the gospel is like this: a father asked his son to fetch some wood from the shed for their stove. The son, whose nose was in a book, didn't respond. The father then became enraged, giving an ultimatum that his son could either obey or leave the house. The son chose the latter, slamming the door on his way out. A fortnight later, the son returned, pleading to be forgiven. The father "softened for a moment. Then he grew stern and, pointing to the woodshed, said, 'Son, that same stick is in the woodshed. Get it, bring it in, put it on the fire, and you can come in.'"[2]

Despite the similar plot points, this story has a very different feel than Jesus's prodigal son story. In Billy Graham's story, it's clear the son has to walk on eggshells to maintain closeness with the father, or else face his wrath. Any little unintentional slipup might erupt into a confrontation that threatens the end of the relationship. Maintaining connection with his father becomes a difficult task, and life at home has an atmosphere of anxiety. This is drastically different from the father who decides to gift his estate, even when the son is impudent. In Jesus's story, the father never asks the son to leave.

We wouldn't feel inclined to share our sadness or worries or pain with the irritable father of Graham's story. And unlike Jesus's returning prodigal, the son in this story can't waltz back into the house to get the closeness he needs. He has to meet some minimum standards of behavior before his father will look at him with love. In the absence of delight, the father places obedience as the foundation of the relationship.

As Graham told this story, he implied how we relate to God. With a Grump Father God, of course we will anxiously monitor closeness, unable to trust that we can get it whenever the need arises. We learn to manage our emotions on our own, afraid we might upset God, who already seems irritable. And we can't expect that our relationship is a secure foundation on which we troubleshoot our behaviors. Instead, we learn that the relationship is precariously balanced upon our conduct, causing us to take extra caution to behave in exactly the right ways.

Research Insight

In 1945, while attachment theory was developing, Paul Johnson, a psychologist of religion, wrote, "The emotional quality of faith is indicated in a basic confidence and security. . . . Without emotional security there is no relaxation, but tension, distress and instability."[3]

With a God like the father in Graham's story, it only makes sense that we'd anxiously try to keep our Divine Parent happy, tiptoeing around as we try to stuff down our fear or doubt or sadness, those feelings that seem to be opposite of the marks of true faith. Of course we would desperately try to change into someone more like Jesus and less like ourselves to gain the acceptance we long for. We want closeness with God, and these are the maps we've been given.

DIFFERENT WAYS OF RELATING TO THE SAME GOD

Some people find God to be a source of strength and comfort.

Others find a relationship with God to be a soul-crushing burden.

Then there's most of us, somewhere in between, experiencing times of comfort and times when we worry that we're doing it all wrong, and God feels far away. Why are there so many ways of relating to the same God?

That's a million-dollar question that psychologists who research spirituality continue to explore. Some believe that our ways of relating to God tend to run down two paths. The first is that of correspondence, where you relate to God in a way similar to your parents. Whether your parents were caring and attentive or harsh and distant, you expect the same from God and end up with an attachment style with God that mirrors how you approached relationship with your parents.

The second path of relating is finding God to be the opposite of your parents, which often occurs in those who grew up without the love and security they needed. In this path, you reach out to God to compensate for the support and love you didn't receive growing up. If your parents were conditional and judgmental but you find that God accepts and loves you unconditionally, you relate to God in a different way than you did with your parents. You find that God gives you the love and care you felt starved of in your early relationships.

However, this line of research has often started with the assumption that our parental experiences are the primary factor in forming how we relate to God. Other research has considered what types of theological teaching encourage different ways of reaching out to God, in healthy and unhealthy ways. One study looked at various denominations and found specific patterns for the ways members reached out to God during times of stress.[4] It's important to look not only at our own family of origin but also the messages we received about God, especially early on in faith.

None of us have received a perfect understanding of God. Our specific relationship with God is built on who we are and our unique experiences. Yes, our parents influence our perception of God. But the church we grew up in, our current faith community, and the dominant theology of our larger culture also affect our relationship with God. Then there's our specific theology and traumatic experiences, as well as our gender, sexual orientation, culture, personality, and psychological health.[5] And of course, our direct experience with God also affects our relationship.

RIPPLES OF A DISTORTED PICTURE

The question of what God is like is not merely an abstract one. When we're given a distorted picture of God, we end up with unhealthy practices that don't impact only our personal lives. How we relate to God affects our systems, our politics, and how we practice our faith in the world. If we anxiously try to keep close by vigilantly making sure we never offend a holy God, we end up valuing rules over people. We hear about asylum seekers at the southern border and we're more upset about laws being broken than about human suffering. We become like the religious leaders of Jesus's day who complained about healing on the Sabbath.

If we can't bring our difficult feelings to God, we end up dealing with them in other ways. We shove them down, which makes it difficult for us to access our emotions when we need them. To engage in empathy, we need to be able to get in touch with our own sadness or fear or pain. If we've locked those away, then we'll struggle to respond compassionately to the suffering we see in the world, whether it's the stories of houseless people in our neighborhood or Nigerians who need clean water. We can't take the risk of their experiences affecting us because of the emotions it might bring up in us.

Lastly, if we can't see the delight that God has in us as beloved children of God, we will also be blind to God's delight in others. We'll fail to see the reflection of God in the eyes of others. When we can't see these things, we run the risk of dehumanizing others, sometimes even in violent ways, all while claiming to love God.

Attachment science is new, but the horrific consequences of failing to see our Divine Parent's love for those who are different from us is as old as time. In my heritage, this has looked like brutal colonization, kidnapping and enslaving Africans, slaughtering Native peoples, and more. Those who have not yet understood their own belovedness will lack the ability to treat others as children of God, with horrific consequences. It's the belief that we must be fundamentally transformed before we are fit for a relationship with God that can drive horrendous American projects like "Kill the Indian in him, save the man."[6] Looking at spirituality through the lens of attachment, we can understand how our faith can be a firm foundation to join with God's mission of healing in the world—or a terrible burden that hurts us and harms others, all depending on the maps we've been given.[7]

What has your heritage given you? Have you been given distorted pictures of God that feel like heavy burdens you can hardly carry?[8] How have these distortions harmed marginalized people or perpetuated injustice, rather than eradicated it? Have you felt the longing for a clear picture of a God who *really* has good news for everyone?

WHAT KIND OF GOD?

Jesus's good news was that God is a better parent than we've been told. His teaching centered on what God was like and how God worked in the world. He addressed important assumptions and questions about God. Does God allow only the most holy close?[9] Does God favor the righteous?[10] Are those who suffer receiving their right punishment?[11] Does God expect strident obedience that burdens those on the edges of society, while creating easy paths for those with means?[12] Were the people of God called to violently overthrow oppressors who have demeaned God and the chosen people?[13] Is God just, and if so, what does God's justice look like?[14]

Jesus came to tell us that God is so much better than we imagined. At the outset, in Luke 4:18–19, Jesus makes his aims clear: to bring good news to the poor, freedom for prisoners and oppressed people, sight for the blind. He came to bring good news to those who suffer most. It is in our suffering that we find the good news.

A CLEARER PICTURE

Pictures fade over time. In the prodigal son parable, Jesus gave us a beautiful picture of God as a secure Parent—some have suggested it'd be better titled "The Forgiving Father," since it's really a story about who God is. But this picture of a loving God can be hard to hold on to.

Jesus himself becomes a picture of God's love on the cross: we, as humanity, do our very worst to our God, who then returns three days later, saying, "Peace be with you."[15] If shame is the feeling that our actions have caused severe relational disconnection, the cross and resurrection shatter our shame. God proves that nothing we do will separate us.

Yet all sorts of distortions have worked their way into this picture. We've been warned to be careful of "a God who is all love, all grace, all mercy"[16] by theologians who worry we might feel too safe with God. We've heard a version of the "good news" that includes the bad news that we are revolting to God. It stains the good news, like a trojan horse, implanting shame in what's supposed to be a balm to our suffering.

Brad Jersak talks about the true gospel as a beautiful masterpiece painting that has been damaged over time with mold and residue. We have to carefully remove what doesn't belong if we're going to see the original picture. We can't voraciously scrape away at it; removing the residue takes care and attentiveness. But where do we begin?

It is in our burdens and pain that we find the questions. Does God want me to feel exhausted trying to keep closeness? Do I have to stuff down my worry and doubt and anger to have true faith? Has my sin made me disgusting to God?

Before you become too worried, I want to be clear that we can't base our theology entirely on our feelings. But everyone interprets Scripture; no one holds the corner on true understanding. And to believe we do is to fall short of the humility that is a part of our faith. Our feelings should drive us to seek to understand God better. It gives us the questions to bring to Scripture, to our communities, and to God in prayer. It helps us integrate a whole faith into our whole beings.

What feelings come up in you during your regular interactions with God, the Bible, and your church? Is there an uncomfortable feeling that comes up over and over? Something that says, "This doesn't quite feel right," or a little pinprick, like a little sting in your heart? You might know this sort of feeling, something you might try to ignore or suppress. What would it be like to pay attention to this pain and approach Scripture hoping to find an answer?

REASONS FOR RECONSIDERATION

Throughout history, we've used scientific discoveries to better understand Scripture. In the sixteenth century, Galileo suggested that the sun was at the center of our universe, which was met with opposition by the church and declared formal heresy. But with time, we understood that statements like "the sun stood still" in Joshua 10:13 needn't be a textbook definition of what occurred, so much as the experience of the people at that time. The church has often struggled with science, but when we use new discoveries as a launching pad to meditate on Scripture and our tradition, we move toward a more robust faith.

Attachment research has shown us clear patterns of healthy parent-child relationship.

- We know that security is built on a relationship that is not dependent on behavior.
- We know that helping your child identify their emotions and manage their inner turmoil is the way to create a safe haven.
- And we know that delighting in your child, communicating—more than anything else—that you love them, is the way to true connection.

So it only makes sense that we would return to the Scriptures and consider the story of a God who throughout history has used parent metaphors to describe the relationship between humanity and the Divine.

Do we see the themes of secure spirituality in these parent metaphors? Can we find good news for our suffering and longings, though perhaps buried under mold and debris? Might we find, in the pages of Scripture, a secure relationship with God?

Chapter Seven

FROM ANXIETY
TO REST

In chapter three we learned that people with an anxious attachment style are like little kids who want so badly to be good, to earn their parents' affection. Anyone with this style will work tirelessly to maintain the closeness they long for. Early on in Bowlby's research, he found a case study that demonstrated this devastating longing for closeness.

Patrick's mother voluntarily placed him in a care home for single-parent families. In Britain during this time period, these were facilities that provided a place for children to live while single parents worked, still allowing the parent to maintain parental rights, visiting whenever they were able. In this system, the family could stay together, in some sense. When she dropped him off at the group home, he was sternly warned to "be a good boy and not to cry—otherwise his mother would not visit him."[1]

The three-year-old boy—whom I imagine with blond hair, blue eyes, and dimples, like my own son—did just that. Determined to hold in his tears, Patrick would instead nod his head whenever anyone looked at him. The day after he was admitted to the nursery, his mother was hospitalized with influenza and was unable to visit Patrick for a week. No one explained this to Patrick, so all he knew was that his mother wasn't visiting him. Each day, he would nod his head over and over, desperately hoping that withholding his tears would bring her back. Each tearless day, he would tell himself, and anyone nearby, "My mother will put on my overcoat and take me home again."[2]

The longer he waited to see his mother, the longer his list of preparation became, as though he could squash down the tears welling up inside by planning for her return. Over and over, he'd repeat, "She will put on my overcoat and my leggings, she will zip up the zipper, she will put on my pixie hat."[3] His endless repetition annoyed the hospital staff, who chastised him and told him to be quiet. Wanting so badly to be a good boy so his mother would come back, Patrick turned his reassurances inward, silently mouthing the list of clothing his mother would put on him before taking him home. In the absence of words, he mimed each piece of clothing, imagining putting on his hat and coat and zipping up the zipper.

With every silent motion, Patrick soldiered on to be the good boy who would earn his mother's return. But in a matter of days, he began to lose hope. His vibrant pantomime slowed into small, lifeless movements. Eventually, while surrounded by other children playing together and making music, Patrick, "totally uninterested, would stand somewhere in a corner, moving his hands and lips with an absolutely tragic expression on his face."[4]

CONNECT, THEN REDIRECT

Patrick tried to be a good boy to get the connection he needed, but it never worked, and his efforts to get the closeness he longed for meant being less himself, trying to contort himself into a perfect kid that could earn his mom's presence. When a relationship is based on behavior, like Patrick's, we will strain ourselves to fall into line in ways that damage who we are and force us to ignore our needs. We endlessly perform for our connection in a way that prevents us from resting and feeling secure. Sometimes we get burned out; sometimes we totally devolve, like Patrick. And sometimes we keep going and going, believing that striving is better than losing connection altogether. But we weren't supposed to operate in relationships this way.

Dr. Tina Payne Bryson and Dr. Dan Siegel created a set of parenting strategies based on attachment and interpersonal neurobiology—the science of how we relate and respond to one another. One strategy they suggest is to "connect, then redirect."[5] In a moment of bad behavior, healthy parents affirm the relationship, and *then* they address the behavior. This helps separate the status of the relationship from behavior, giving the child the message that closeness is not contingent on what they do.[6]

The practical side of this is that when a parent connects with their child, it calms the child's nervous system. This might look like getting down on their knees and meeting the child's eyes, face-to-face. Usually in children—and often with adults—bad behavior comes when they're emotionally overwhelmed. When we have a secure relationship to stand on, we usually make better choices. Also, when a parent helps their child calm down, they can discuss the behavior, which makes the child less likely to repeat it in the future. Siegel and Bryson are "not recommending permissiveness or letting your boundaries slide,"[7] but simply suggesting that there are ways to maintain connection through it all. Once a child is calm, they can talk about what to do differently next time or how to make amends. Because we have a hard time taking in information when we're overwhelmed with emotion, Seigel and Bryson write, "It's generally a good idea to discuss misbehavior and its consequences after the child has calmed down."[8]

The best part of this method is that it creates a security beneath the behavior. By connecting with a child, especially in a moment of conflict or bad behavior, they learn that their behavior does not sway the relationship, creating emotional safety. They can truly rest in the relationship, without fear that their misbehavior will jeopardize closeness. And when we look at the story of Scripture, we see that God does the same with people.

SEPARATED BY SIN

Perhaps you've heard that sin separates us from God. You may have been told that the only way to end the separation and get close to God is through the punishment of sin. But the Bible tells another story.

God creates the first two humans, and within two short chapters, they are tempted by a serpent and commit humankind's first sin. That same day, God comes to walk with them in the cool of the evening, presumably no different from any other evening, but Adam and Eve hide. God calls for them, finds them, and has a conversation—not yelling across cliffs, but in their presence. Of course there are consequences, but we find that God remains with them, even outside the garden. Many theologians believe that withholding the Tree of Life was vital to the well-being of Adam and Eve, not a punitive measure. It was a healthy boundary.

One chapter later, Cain kills Abel, his own brother—a sin that would separate a person from God if there ever was one. But actually, it seems to draw God close. Yahweh shows up and talks with Cain.[9] Later, Jacob cheats Esau out of his birthright and deceives his father. Yet he ends up meeting God in the desert.[10] In the second book of the Bible, Moses kills a man and flees the city, only later to be met by God in a burning bush.[11] The apostle Paul, during his life as Saul, kills Christians, and then is met by Jesus on the road to Damascus.[12] God continually approaches us, even at our worst moments.

Admittedly, connection with God is not all sunshine and roses. Adam and Eve have to relocate. God informs Cain that he is under a curse, coming from his brother's blood. Jacob wrestles with God. Moses is called into a liberation movement he doesn't feel prepared for. Paul is blinded for three days. However, we see that God is not driven away by sin but instead engages with people and their sin. We see a God that connects, then redirects. Never in any of these stories do we hear that the relationship is ever in jeopardy. Perceived feelings of closeness may shift—we will go through the mountains and valleys—but with these possible shifts in mind, we can still know that our relationship is intact.

When you see that not even murder separates God from his people, you can begin to relax your grip on the balloon. You can begin to take a breath. When you don't desperately have to keep God close, you can splay out on the lap of a Divine Parent and experience the peace we've been promised. You can find the emotional safety of a secure relationship that does not sway with your behavior.

FAMILY RULES

Healthy families have rules for living together, but those rules are not the basis of belonging. My family has our basic ground rules on the fridge, the "Ten Commandments of the Mayfield house," you could say. Within this set of rules are consequences like time-outs and losing privileges, as well as ways to make amends. They are an important part of teaching my kids—and reminding myself—how to respect and love others, how to repair when we've wronged someone else, and how to have appropriate boundaries within relationships. In our family, we use kind words, and we don't use our bodies to hurt others. When we've hurt someone else, we apologize and try to make it as right as possible.

But these rules have nothing to do with belonging. I'm not going to kick my kids out of the house if they don't follow the rules. The rules exist for my kids to learn how to engage in healthy relationships, and so that each person will be valued and respected. My wife and I try to teach them that *secure relationships are based in the felt safety of knowing there may be ups and downs, even times of distance, but the relationship itself is never in jeopardy.*

As they learn that belonging and connection don't hinge on following the rules, they will relax into a relationship with me and my wife that gives them security. They won't feel like they have to walk on eggshells, because there's room for mistakes in our secure relationship. We hope they will feel loved, knowing they are accepted, especially when they're far from perfect. It doesn't mean there aren't consequences, but their relationship with us is never in danger.

THE LAW

The "family rules" approach mirrors how God has approached people throughout the span of Scripture. Jesus, grieved by Jerusalem's murderous response to prophet after prophet who called them to better behavior, still longed to gather them "together, as a hen gathers her chicks under her wings."[13] In letters the apostle Paul wrote to the early churches, he regularly begins by affirming their status as members of the family, referring to them as brothers and sisters,[14] children of God,[15] and sometimes even "as my beloved children"[16] before talking to them about their behavior. And God states that the Mosaic law was given for Israel's own good, not to determine who was considered in and who was out.[17]

Unfortunately, many of us have not been given a picture of a Divine Parent whose relationship does not sway based on our behavior. Even certain passages of Scripture seem to show us a picture of a wrathful, jealous God who threatens destruction to Israel and the surrounding nations. And yet a careful reading of the story shows that even when God's wrath flares, it is accompanied by promises of healing and restoration. God delivers Israel into exile yet responds to their needs and cares for them throughout the process.

God even shows this pattern of enduring connection to foreign nations. In Isaiah 19, God first promises to bring wrath upon Egypt, proclaiming, "They will shudder with fear at the uplifted hand that the LORD Almighty raises against them."[18] But later, in the same chapter, God responds to Egypt's cries and heals them, and they will be considered a blessing to the earth, alongside Israel and Assyria. God declares, "Blessed be Egypt my people, Assyria my handiwork, and Israel my inheritance."[19]

When you're given a picture of a wrathful God that is absent of the healing resolution as seen in passages like Isaiah 19, it's further evidence that you can't relax with God. Unfortunately, sometimes even Jesus's death—a picture of God's mercy and grace—can become a subtle reminder of a perfectionist God who is just waiting to punish you. And it's hard to rest in the arms of a God like that. It never allows you to experience a safety that is deeper than how we act. When you have this picture of God, you have to cling, fretting about your closeness.

I have worked with many clients who grew up in homes where near-impossible standards were held over their heads. These standards sprout from a variety of circumstances: some parents want their children to survive in a dog-eat-dog world. Other parents can't bear the shame that failure would bring on the family or the shame that wells up when their children don't measure up. Others don't even know that their standards are so harsh, simply passing on the legacy they received from their own parents.

And within that group of clients, there form two groups: those who succeed at meeting those standards and those who fail to meet them. But at the end of the day, they all fall in the same category because, whether they succeed or fail, they are still starving for connection. They long to move from anxiety to rest. Meeting a standard is vastly different from living in a relationship where you are loved no matter what. Approval is not the same as connection.

Some of us have been given a picture of a God whose acceptance of us is contingent on our rigidly following a long list of rules. This costs us not only the chance to rest in the arms of a loving God but also the ability to see the Old Testament law as a good gift from the generous heart of God. Contrary to what we've been told, this law comes not from a demanding exacting judge but the doting heart of a parent who wants the best for us. To truly relax with God, we need a better understanding of the law and also God's promises to people. It might be helpful to understand where this picture of a perfectionist God came from.

A DEMANDING PARENT

While a picture of a harsh and strict God existed long before Martin Luther, it was during the Reformation in the sixteenth century when this view was really cemented. God's law was seen as prerequisite for acceptance, and the failure to uphold every rule resulted in punishment from a dictatorial God—a punishment Jesus endured in his death. As a result, the Protestant church lost the view of the law as a gift to the people of God. In most churches, mere reference to the law elicits images of a perfectionistic and demanding God who is waiting for us to fail. What we believe about law is important because it reflects what we believe about the God who gave it. But how did we end up with this view of law?

Martin Luther appears to have had an anxious attachment in his relationship to God. One way he tried to keep God close was the endless confession of sin, "marathon sessions, dragging on for hours and hours. No sin was too small, no transgression too insignificant, and no error of thought or questionable expression of emotion could be overlooked."[20] A constant nagging voice in his head told him that he needed to either follow every single command or confess what he did not follow. Sometimes he would finish a long session of confession only to find that on the way back to his room, he had sinned again or recognized something he'd missed and would stop in his tracks, turn around, and return to the confessional. He came to resent this God that demanded perfection. He wrote, "I hated those words, 'the righteousness of God,' and more, I did not love, indeed I hated, that God who punished sinners . . . secretly I was angry with God."[21] He was exhausted from and resentful of a God who demanded complete purity for connection.

So when Luther created a theology that would endure for centuries beyond him in the Protestant tradition, he found the Old Testament law to be similar to that nagging voice in his head. He believed that the law was a set of demands that determined whether God accepted us and would get close. If we get close to God by following the rules, then the Old Testament law was an overwhelming burden of 613 rules to follow.

Luther also projected his own anxiety and guilt into Paul's letters to the early church. He assumed that, like him, Paul felt crushed by the hundreds of laws and that Jesus's work on the cross abolished the law and wiped his conscience clean. The law had become an enemy that nagged at Luther day and night. He found peace in the idea that through faith, he is no longer held to law. He believed law to be the exact opposite of God's grace. But that's not what the law was intended to be in the first place.

RULES ON THE FRIDGE

Just like the rules on the fridge in our house, God gave the law so that the chosen nation would know how to relate to each other in healthy ways that upheld the *imago Dei* in each person. Wilda Gafney, in her book *Womanist Midrash*, writes that the law "is simply (and not so simply) a text about how to live in relationship: how to live in relationship to God and how to live in relationship to others in the community."[22] Acceptance into God's community was not dependent on following the law; the law was given because of being accepted into community. Sort of like, "We're a family, so let's talk about how we're going to live together."

The law existed to "help to maintain proper boundaries and categories and, in so doing, maintain the health of the community and its individuals."[23] God wanted a community where the marginalized were taken care of, fairness was displayed among individuals and communities, and ways were established to make amends when people inevitably harmed one another.

God gave [the law] not to keep himself happy, or to take pleasure in finding fault with Israel's failures, but for its own good. They urged one another to obey it, not in order to get saved, but because God had already saved them.[24]
—Stephen Burnhope

We've mistakenly believed we need to follow the law to be accepted by God and missed out on understanding that it was given for our good. Jesus makes this clear when he speaks of one of the Ten Commandments that perhaps impacted Jewish life most frequently: Sabbath. While most of the commands were "thou shalt nots," a discouragement from certain behaviors, Sabbath was a regular practice that required preparation and interrupted the regular day to day. Yet as we discussed earlier, Jesus assures us that practicing the Sabbath is not to keep God happy; it's for our well-being: "The Sabbath was made for man, not man for the Sabbath," he says.[25]

Instead of a God who offers rest, we've ended up with a rigid God who gets angry the moment we step out of line, or pulls away when we don't live up to his standards. But the very fact that there were atonement sacrifices was a big indication that God did not expect people to follow the law perfectly. Contrary to Luther's interpretation, recent scholarship has found that Israel likely approached the laws as general "guidelines" that pointed them in the way of true justice and health, rather than something to be rigidly followed. Just as the rules on our fridge at home aren't about appeasing the parents—they're about teaching my kids how to live in loving ways together. Sometimes we have to find an alternative solution that is in the spirit of the rules and don't follow them exactly.

Summarizing significant scholarship on the Jewish law, Tim Mackie and Jon Collins at BibleProject produced a series of videos and podcasts to help us better understand how Israel understood the purpose of the law.[26] They've suggested that we're best off reading the law as God-given wisdom. God outlines these ways of living to create a society that works together toward the flourishing of all people. The law pointed Israel in the direction of health and wholeness, toward a way of living together that cares for the vulnerable and ensures fairness.

God does seem to be regularly frustrated and even angry with the chosen people. As a parent myself, I can say that frustration is a part of the everyday life of parenting. In Jeremiah 31, God talks about frustration with one of the tribes of Israel but then, within a few sentences, wants them close again: "Though I often speak against him . . . my heart yearns for him" (v. 20). Anyone with kids can relate. One minute they're driving us crazy, the next, we look in their eyes and they melt our hearts. Underlying everything is God's love for people.

When we begin to see that even prior to Jesus's work, God never based connection on behavior, we can relax a little. And if we know that God doesn't run away from our sin, we can ask for help in the spots we get stuck.

COVENANT: UNCONDITIONAL AND CONDITIONAL

Covenant is a word God often uses to describe how he relates to people, and it's usually a word that means agreement or contract. "I'll do this if you do that." But let me tell you, God has a strange idea of how contracts work.

In Exodus 19:5–6, God is bringing Israel out of Egypt and establishing a new nation, an inauguration of a country under the kingship of Yahweh. God tells the people, "If you obey me fully and keep my covenant, then out of all nations you will be my treasured possession." He clarifies that "the whole earth is mine" but that Israel specifically will be "a kingdom of priests and a holy nation."

On its face, it looks like closeness is dependent on our behavior.

We read this declaration, and our anxious spirituality kicks into gear as we worry whether we've obeyed enough to remain God's treasured possession. But if we keep reading the story, we find that Israel continually fails to obey God fully—and yet God never withdraws or abandons them. We see divine anger at times, and there are certainly parts in the story when they are punished, but God never gives up. Theologian Miroslav Volf wrote, "Israel is irrevocably elect and immutably loved by God; no failure on Israel's part can change this."[27] They are the chosen people, and no amount of bad behavior can alter that part of the relationship.

Then there's the part of Israel being a "holy nation." *Holy* doesn't always mean impeccably pure; it can mean set apart for a specific role: the goal of creating a society that reflects the justice, mercy, and love at the heart of God. If Israel does not follow the guidance given, they will not be able to create such a society and won't succeed in reflecting a holy God in a world of injustice. This inability has nothing to do with God's action but is simply the natural consequence of falling short of living into God's wisdom.

Basing their understanding primarily on Leviticus 19–21, many readers assume that by keeping the law Israel would thereby become holy. . . . Many today likewise think that we are to pursue holiness (the same piety and morality) by obeying the same rules in order to achieve holiness. This is mistaken and misses the point. . . . God declares his people holy by election decree. It is a status that he gives, and it cannot be gained or lost by the Israelites' own efforts or failures.[28]

—John H. Walton and J. Harvey Walton

It's like the rules on my fridge. If my wife and I say, "We're going to follow these rules so that we live together in healthy, respectful ways," and then my kids aren't respectful of each other, we will fail in our goal to be a healthy family. But it doesn't mean they are no longer my kids. The rules have everything to do with being a member of the family and nothing to do with being a member of the family, all at once. I think this is what Old Testament theologian Walter Brueggemann meant when he wrote, "This covenant relation is characteristically conditional and unconditional at the same time."[29] God never gives up on his people, even as they fail time and time again to listen to his wisdom that will bring peace, justice, and healing to their community in a way that accurately represents the heart of God.

Paul clarifies the role of law when he writes to the Galatians: "If the inheritance depends on the law, then it no longer depends on the promise; but God in his grace gave it to Abraham through a promise."[30]

If you believe your acceptance is based on following rules, you discredit God's gracious gift of unconditional love that has nothing to do with merit. With an anxious attachment style, we try to get close to God through obeying the rules and keeping track of how righteous or unrighteous we are. Paul says that God's commitment to us has nothing to do with following the rules and everything to do with his grace.

We have all failed, not only because we have sinned, but because we have thought it wise to keep tabs at all.[31]
—Danielle Shroyer

Jesus told us about a new covenant that was inaugurated by a meal and a sacrifice—both of his own body. After his resurrection he made his covenant clear: "Surely I am with you always, to the very end of the age."[32] Jesus's statement echoes God's continual assurance to Israel: "I will never leave you nor forsake you."[33] God has every right to pull out of the agreement—and yet never does. God's love is unconditional, and the law is a gift of wisdom toward life and health. When we believe it to be a list of rules that gets us close to God, we miss the experience of God's grace and unconditional love.

The "rules" are important, but not to avoid disconnection or punishment. It can be easy to end up feeling as though you're suffering under an angry tyrant, resentfully following the rules in an effort to avoid abandonment. But this isn't the reason God has given commandments throughout Scripture. They are a gift given for human flourishing and healthy communities.

Commandment Exercise

1. Think about some commandments you follow in your walk with God. Jot down five of them, such as:
   - being honest with my words and actions[34]
   - caring for the least of these[35]
   - being faithful to my spouse[36]
2. Take time to meditate on each of these commandments you try to follow, and consider the ways they are helpful to you and those you know. Rather than these commandments —this Divine wisdom—being a demand that we show God our love, consider how they might show God's love for you, those you love, and the most vulnerable in your community. Consider

the natural consequences of suffering that could happen without this guidance.

3. Now reframe each commandment into a statement about God's wishes for you and for the world:

- "God wants me to be in a healthy community where people treat each other well and trust one another."
- "God wants the poor and sick—people made in God's image—to be cared for."
- "God wants my marriage to be an emotionally safe place of refuge."

4. Lastly, take two minutes to consider these statements and what they say about God's attitude toward you.

MONUMENTS

It may be hard for you to relax and feel secure with God.

If you've grown up with a theology that told you that God is close only when you behave yourself, it might seem impossible ever to get close. You might try to learn better theology, or memorize verses like Romans 8:38–39 that remind you that nothing can separate you from the love of God, or that God promises, "Never will I leave you; never will I forsake you."[37] But your relational brain and attachment system don't change with merely more data. Learning more information about God doesn't always work the way you wish it did. God understands that it's hard to believe how much you are loved. You've been given many needling messages that discredit God's love, many sentences that start with "God loves you but," that have whittled away at your belovedness.

God knows about our brains. We are relational beings who need more than just words; we thrive on experience and images. The book of Joshua tells the story where Israel comes up against the Jordan River and God parts the water for them to cross through. God then instructs them to build a monument of twelve stones as a reminder of his kindness to them. While other nations were constructing graven images to glorify their gods, the God of Israel asked them to construct a memorial not only for glory but to remind the people of God's unending parental care and to signal to the other nations that Israel had a God who watched over them.[38]

Likewise, Jesus's Last Supper shows us that he understands that we need more than words to experience God's love and truth. Jesus tells us to eat and remember. It's a spiritual practice that we hold with our hands, taste with our mouths, and take into our bodies. It reminds us that our sin will never separate us from God and that closeness is not dependent on our being good enough. We are given not only an abstract truth, we are given symbols of God's unending love that we can hold on to and engage with, in community.

A BETTER PICTURE OF GOD

It's important to find concrete reminders of God's love that we can hold on to, especially when we become anxious about our standing with the Divine. Our brains don't often respond to black-and-white statements; they need help experiencing the colorful love of God. We need messages of security that resonate with our hearts, not only our heads. Often what helps us concretely remember God's love is unique to each person.

Bread and wine don't always convey God's message of "I love you forever" to everyone, nor does a pile of rocks, but they are examples of God using concrete symbols to remind us of his unending love. I believe this gives us license to do the same.

A few years ago, I was facing a lot of the ugly pictures of God I'd been given. I woke up one morning with a sense that God was utterly disgusted with me and that our relationship was hanging in the balance. At the suggestion of my wife, I went to a nearby Catholic garden called The Grotto. There I saw a statue of Mary holding baby Jesus against her chest.

I don't often hear the voice of God, but there have been a few times that I think I have—this was one of those times. I looked at the statue of Mary holding Jesus, and I clearly understood God saying to me, *That's like you and me. You can cry on my chest whenever you need, and I'll hold you close.* It wasn't an audible voice but something I heard. To be honest, at first I wasn't sure I could trust that it was God speaking.

So I spat back, *That doesn't fit with real theology. You are a father, and you are constantly judging me, and I am so tired of it!*

I'm your mother now, God said, *and you can cry on my chest whenever you need. I know you're so tired and sad and feel so bad about yourself.* I softened a little, walked farther, and eventually found myself in a small chapel, nestled on the side of a hill that overlooked northeast Portland. One wall was entirely windows, and the rest of the room was marble. I sank into a large, puffy chair. Then, not unlike some characters in the Bible, I said, *But I need to know for sure—can you give me an image I can cling to? Please, I need something concrete.*

At that moment, a woman walked in holding a baby that instantly started howling. Out of the corner of my eye, I could see the mother bobbing her knees, tenderly looking into her baby's eyes, softly singing.

Okay, I said. I understood this was the picture to hang on to, and it turned out to be the exact thing I needed. In fact, I was skeptical of the voice precisely because I needed it so badly. I could barely dare to hope it could be true. God as a mother holding me felt different, very different, from the God I'd known my whole life. It created a sense of safety that I could feel in my body. Even without the physical touch that can create safety, something within me changed. Something within our relationship changed. I could rest.

YOUR PERSONAL MONUMENTS

For those of us who have clung to God like a balloon threatening to float away, it's difficult to believe in God's consistent love when we're not constantly engaged in our regular spiritual practices or when we find ourselves sinning repeatedly. Many spiritual maps tell us that God *cannot* be close to us when we're sinning or when we're not constantly grasping for closeness.

When the sense of abandonment registers as a threat to our brains, we need something that will calm us down. We already know theological statements about God's love, but they don't help the way we'd like. Our internal alarms go off, and we don't know how to remind ourselves that God is close no matter what. Even as we recite Bible verses, we think of all the what-ifs and caveats to God's grace we've been told about. *It's important during these times to have your own monuments that can help you hold on to the truth that God has a covenant with you to stay close forever.* You need experiential ways of understanding God's love. Sometimes it's a painting like Rembrandt's *Prodigal Son* or a particular song with a line that sinks into your heart. Perhaps it's a liturgy or spiritual practice that brings you a sense of calm. Maybe it's an image or simply a word.

April, whom I talked about in chapter 3, found that in her many years of study, God had given her countless pictures of unending kindness. I suggested, rather than striving for the next truth, that she engage in a practice that Israel often did: reflecting on what God has done in the past. She spent time looking through her many notebooks to find some of the biblical truths that had brought that feeling of closeness alive in her. Not surprisingly, many of them were images or metaphors. She spent time creating artwork that represented these important truths and placed them in prominent places. Rather than an endless search for the next truth, she could relax in gratefulness for the truths she'd found in God's Word—and then spend some time resting her brain rather than pushing it to find the next bit of information buried in Scripture.

Try this exercise in building your own monument. Let it remind you of God's closeness.

—— Monument Exercise ——

In our lives, I hope most of us have times of poignantly experiencing joy, peace, love, and acceptance. They often surprise us—and then pass quickly. Take a moment to find your own monument to God's love.

1. Identify a time you've felt safe or loved or calm or felt God's presence.
2. Is there a concrete reminder of that time? A picture, song, poem, or other object you can return to?
3. If not, can you draw or create an image that reminds you of the experience?
4. Take this reminder and place it somewhere you'll regularly see it.
5. This helps the emotional right side of your brain integrate the left-brained logical statements you know about God's love.

RELAXING YOUR GRIP

Love is hard to find and often comes with conditions. It's natural to long for a relationship where you can stop striving. When you don't have to grasp anxiously at God for closeness, you can feel a little calmer. Your nervous system can even relax as you unwind into the safe invisible arms of a God who will never leave.

When you can relax into God's arms, you can begin to look outside your little clingy circle of anxiety. You can rest deeply and wake to join with God's mission to heal the world. You'll find that as your brain space is no longer filled with desperation to get close to God, you can be more open to thinking of others, listening to the suffering of the world, being present with those you love and present with yourself. You can also be more present with God, open to the rest your Divine Parent provides. You can live in the way humans were created to.

After spending decades of working tirelessly to keep God close, I came across a portion of a poem that became one of my "monuments." It's from a centuries-old poem by Persian poet Hafiz titled "Your Mother and My Mother," which talks about God's desire for playfulness in our lives.

I wrote it down and posted it in my office where only I could see it. It was a constant reminder that God created me for joy and connection and playfulness, things that can easily evaporate when I find myself toiling to keep God close.

The poem brings to my mind a secure toddler who doesn't have to cling to his mom's skirt. Imagine it: he skips around the park, singing to himself, poking at bugs, looking at shapes in the clouds. He gives glory to God simply by doing exactly what he was created to do—to play and learn and marvel at God's wonderful world. And the stable relationship with his mother empowers him to do it.

And just as the secure, care-free toddler feels free with his mom, God also wants to give you this freedom and peace and joy as you lean on the everlasting arms.

Chapter Eight

FROM SHUTDOWN
TO ENGAGED

Something important happens right at the beginning of the Bible, though we're prone to overlook it. In the second verse, in a moment between the world being created and God separating dark from light, we are told that the Spirit of God hovers over the waters, suspended over the depths.

When I was a kid, I hated thinking about the deep. We'd be on a riverbank, and my dad would explain that the river was as deep as a two-story house was high, and all I could imagine was an entire house being swallowed into the murky water and all the unknown creatures that lived between the surface and the riverbed. It's no surprise I feared the river, as my grandfather drowned in a river just two months before I was born, taken by the current to have his breath and life extinguished. I grew up in a town where the river was the hub of activity, but I never was comfortable with the water because of what my mind could imagine.

Ancient Israel had a similar relationship to bodies of water.

The depths were always a metaphorical nod to the chaos of the world. So the beginning of the world is this: God is present with the turbulent chaos—and then calms it. Many ancient religons had stories of their gods creating the world, but it was Israel's God that ushered in a calm in which humankind, animals, and plants would thrive in peaceful community.

The gospel writers tell the story of the same world-ordering God embodied in Jesus. One stormy night at sea, the disciples are crossing the Sea of Galilee while Jesus sleeps in the boat, and the waves toss the boat back and forth. In his book, *In the Shelter*, Pádraig Ó Tuama writes as only a poet would: "All they knew was their feeling, and their feeling was the unsteady wood beneath their feet: wood of a boat on an uncertain sea."[1] The disciples wake Jesus, wondering if he even cares about their well-being. Then, in the simplest of sentences, Jesus calms the sea with three words: "Quiet! Be still!"[2] And he does again what was done in the beginning, bringing order to chaos.

When we're children, our internal worlds can be overwhelming, and like the disciples, we need to know we are not alone and that someone cares. We need someone to speak calmly to help us still the swirling waters within. According to neuroscientists, when a parent notices and names an emotion, its impact is reduced significantly.[3] Dan Siegel and Tina Payne Bryson suggest employing this as a simple parenting technique: "name it to tame it."[4] That means that feeling of sadness or worry or anger tends to be less overwhelming when we've identified what we're feeling and, ideally, share it with someone we're close to. Think about it, when you have a tough day at work and you get a chance to tell someone about it—someone who really listens and cares for you—you feel better. Simply being heard helps us calm down.

Siegel uses the term "feeling felt," which is when we know that our feelings resonate with someone else.[5] It happens when we see our internal world reflected in the eyes of someone we love. This is true connection. We "feel felt" when we know that those we love see and accept our emotions. It creates a little refuge of emotional safety in a harsh world. Feeling felt helps us experience the closeness we long for while also taming our overwhelming emotions.

God longs to engage with you in your emotions because that is where intimacy happens. God invites you to share what's going on inside, even if you don't understand it or even know exactly what's going on inside the basement of your heart. You are summoned into a safe haven where you are seen and understood. As we saw in chapter 4, this invitation has been stifled in many faith communities, obscuring the picture of a God who is waiting to help you order your internal chaos through simply being with you, as a parent does with their upset child.

THE GOD WHO SEES

I want to tell you a story about feeling felt with God, but it includes a difficult part of my story. It's nothing graphic, but certainly traumatic, and sadly it is likely to resonate in some way with many who read this. So I wanted to let you know ahead of time that this next story might be a difficult read for those of you who have been abused or know someone close to you who has.

I am a survivor of sexual abuse, and perhaps the most difficult part of that experience has been what it has meant for relationships within my family. The perpetrator is someone I was close to growing up, someone my family trusted. This scenario is exceedingly common, despite our societal pictures of mustachioed strangers hiding in bushes near playgrounds. In the absence of accountability or resolution, this injury hung over my family dynamics for many years.

And then my grandma died.

Without a doubt, I knew that the person who had abused me would be present at the funeral. I talked it through with my wife. We could drive the five hours down the interstate and five hours back all in one day. Should we? I didn't want to stay long, but I did want to be there for my grandmother's memorial.

So we did. And it was difficult. The person who abused me was present, and throughout the different settings—graveside, sanctuary, church event space, Grandma's house—I spent most of my energy dancing around the room, avoiding contact with this person, with limited success. That was on top of trying to grieve in the midst of all the family dynamics. It was one of the more challenging days of my life, and by the end of it, I was utterly exhausted. I didn't even mind the five-hour drive home to be back in a community where I felt safe and supported.

The next morning we attended a church service, not our church, but the church where my father-in-law pastored at the time, since he and my mother-in-law had watched our daughter during our trip. I remember sitting in the front of the sanctuary, and during the songs I heard the soft voice of God. At that moment, I would've liked some encouragement from God: *Great job! You're awesome! You are so brave!*

But I received something better. Sitting there with my heart feeling so raw, I heard the most soothing voice say, *That was really hard*. I instantly began to weep. I didn't feel like God was proud of me, which was fine because I didn't need an opinion of my performance. I needed to feel felt. And I did. I knew that God saw me and my pain. I knew my pain mattered, that I mattered and could rest in that communion.

According to the Christian tradition, the first person to name God was another victim of abuse, a woman named Hagar. In Genesis, Abram and his wife, Sarai, are worried about the lineage God had promised them. Sarai can't seem to become pregnant, so Abram has sex with Sarai's slave Hagar. Hagar becomes pregnant, and it's not long before conflict arises between her and Sarai. Sarai abuses her, and then Hagar flees to the desert. It is there, in the desert, that a runaway slave woman meets God and names the Divine for the first time.

She calls God "El Roi," which means "the God who sees." Hagar, who feels felt, says, "I have now seen the One who sees me."[6] She knows that she matters to God, having a sense that her experience resonates with God, and she feels the resonance. She feels a connection of closeness and care. Here we learn the story of a God who yearns to draw close and be with us in our turbulent times.

HONEST PRAYERS

God wants to create a sanctuary for honest prayers, where pretense and formalities fall away in favor of true intimacy. As C. S. Lewis writes about prayer, "We must lay before Him what is in us, not what ought to be in us."[7] Sharing what we feel, not what we wish we felt, is the path to security with God.

We move from shutdown to engagement when we share with God what's truly going on inside.

Elijah is one of many examples of emotional honesty with God. On the run from a violent royal family, he prays suicidal prayers, asking God to take his life. All at once, Scripture says, an angel appears and gives him food and water.[8] Through his honest despair, he invites God to respond. True intimacy happens when we can share what's in the basement. Sometimes this even means sharing the anger we have toward God. Jeremiah, tired of his job as a destruction-proclaiming prophet is frustrated with God and tells him directly, "You deceived me, LORD, and I was deceived; you overpowered me and prevailed."[9] He feels like God tricked him, and he complains about it, left in the biblical record to be read for millennia, showing us that we can do the same.

Attachment researchers have found that in a situation where a parent and toddler were briefly separated, parents of secure toddlers did something particular upon their return.[10] They not only showed concern for their child's experience of sadness but also asked *explicitly* about their anger about feeling abandoned. They picked them up and said things like, "Oh, I bet you were so mad when Mommy left, weren't you?" We see that healthy parents make room for anger and affirm it—even when it's against themselves. I think this illuminates, at least in part, one reason that God has preserved records of anger and feelings of abandonment throughout Scripture. It's simply what good parents do: they make room for the negative emotions.

The psalmist writes, "Why, LORD, do you stand far off? Why do you hide yourself in times of trouble?"[11] and later, "How long, LORD? Will you forget me forever? How long will you hide your face from me?"[12] Like a toddler left at daycare, he is angry about the distance he feels. Even Jesus, stepping into our human experience of abandonment, says, "My God, my God, why have you forsaken me?" as he hangs on the cross.[13] These demonstrations of anger and despair lead into honest communication with God. As with a healthy parent, God wants to know about our rage or sadness, and to comfort us in it. This can happen only when we open the basement to our uncomfortable feelings. But looking into these emotions makes sense only when we know that God will embrace them rather than be offended by them.

If you pay attention, you'll notice that many of the Psalms that express anger and feelings of abandonment, including the ones I referenced before, end with hope. Regrettably, however, this format has been abused to further shut down uncomfortable emotions. "Yes, David feels hopeless," a pastor might say, "but in the end, he puts his faith in God," as though David's hopelessness is now void because of his faith. In our black-and-white thinking, we interpret this to mean that David's trust in God eradicated his hopelessness. But this approach robs us of the ability to see what is so important about these psalms: *the psalmist simultaneously holds both his emotions and his faith, one in each hand.* He doesn't have to choose between anger and closeness or sadness and connection. His secure relationship with God can withstand any turbulent emotions that come up. It's not through smothering feelings in faith that he manages them; it is through bringing them forth to God. We don't need to stuff down our feelings; we need to connect with someone who cares about us. We have a Divine Parent who listens to and empathizes with our emotions. A better strategy than shoving our feelings into the basement is sharing them, but we need to know first that they will be accepted.

LOST LAMENT

You can get close to God by expressing your emotions—even your most difficult ones. The notion that difficult emotions should be suppressed before God was a foreign concept to the biblical writers. Lamentations is an entire book of the Bible based on what it sounds like: lamenting. It's a book of poems grieving the destruction of Jerusalem, and Israel finds itself in the midst of incredible loss and shame. The personified city "bitterly . . . weeps at night,"[14] and her "eyes overflow with tears."[15]

"The American church avoids lament," wrote Soong-Chan Rah.[16] We engage our shutdown strategies, focusing primarily on what has gone well—the healings, the transformations, the answered prayers—while striving to keep all the bad stuff in the basement. Rah said this "praise-only narrative is perpetuated by the absence of lament."[17] "Praise-only" is a good term for it: think about the general key and mood of most worship services, or turn to your local Christian radio station, most of which have taglines like "positive," "uplifting," and "wholesome." It's hard to find space for lament or other uncomfortable emotions.

Four of every ten Psalms include lament—nearly half. Yet a study found that only about four out of every hundred hymns in contemporary hymnals lead us in lament.[18] Walter Brueggemann argues that without lament, we lose the ability to enter into real connection with God. Without lament we can only "accept guilt where life with God does not function properly,"[19] leading us into "faith which is based in fear and guilt and lived out as resentful or self-deceptive works of righteousness."[20] In other words, if to stay in God's favor we are always praising and never lamenting, we can't have intimacy with the Divine. Only when we share what is truly within us can we engage in authentic relationship with God. In an emotionally intimate relationship we can find true hope because "hope is forged out of the biblical call to dig deep into our innards," as Dr. Emilie Townes writes, "to tell the truth of what we see, feel, hear, and experience."[21]

You will lose more than intimacy if churches overemphasize the positive aspects of the life of faith. This praise-only approach also drowns out the quiet voices of suffering in our midst. I've heard countless stories of those afflicted with trauma, depression, job loss, family conflict, and more who feel out of place and further disconnected on Sunday mornings in a room full of resplendent celebration. Suppressing the uncomfortable emotions of life keeps the church from seeing the cries of the wounded that we are called to care for and makes those who are suffering feel like outsiders in the family of God.

Israel's holy writings included plenty of complaints. It's a beautiful tradition of emotional engagement. Are the worship services you attend joining in this tradition? Do they make room for your uncomfortable emotions as part of forming a healthy community? Are all voices heard—including those who are sad or suffering? Is your church a place where you can bring your full array of emotions?

Sharing some of your uncomfortable emotions with God might feel strange. But you *can* unlock the basement when you're assured that both God and your faith tradition can hold the parts of your experience. When you are sad, scared, or angry, your emotions aren't signs of a lack of faith, but rather evidence that you are exactly where you need to be—at home with a God who is waiting to hear your emotions and give you the reassurance you need.

Writing a Lament

Lament is a prayer to God that includes both complaint and praise. Take time to follow these steps, writing down each part, and join in the tradition of the psalms:

1. Tell God something you wish were different in your own life or the world, such as a health condition, difficult relationship, life stress, poverty, or racism.

    Example: God, I know there are children who do not have the food they need right now.

2. Next, tell God what you feel when you think about this issue; additionally, write down any emotions you might feel considering God's inaction regarding this issue.

    I feel sad and frustrated that you see it all, and you still let it happen.

3. Tell about a time in your own life or someone else's where God intervened.

    I know you fed the five thousand and gave the Israelites manna in the desert.

4. Ask God to step in and address this suffering.

    Please rescue starving children globally and in my own community.

5. Tell God you're confident that your prayer is heard.

    I know you hear my prayer and that you care about children.

6. Praise or recognize one of God's attributes or characteristics, based on your past or present experience.

    You are the God who fills the hungry with good things and sends the rich away empty. I praise you for your loving justice.

DON'T BE AFRAID

Don't be afraid is one of the most abused phrases from the Bible. If you have a shutdown attachment style, these words— one of the most caring phrases God ever utters—can become twisted and misunderstood. It's almost as if the Bible agrees with your desire to shut down your emotions. But that is not the case.

Throughout Scripture, God repeatedly says, "Do not be afraid," at least fifty times. It's also an opening statement for angels (which might say something about how terrifying angels look, more than anything else). Jesus himself says, "Do not worry,"[22] and the apostle Paul clearly says, "Do not be anxious about anything."[23] Over and over, we are told not to worry or fear. There are commands such as "do not let your hearts be troubled."[24] Without a vision of an emotionally engaged God, we read these statements as a cold, strict ban on emotion rather than words of reassurance and invitation to safety.

But I believe these words aren't all that different from the way I comfort my son when he's scared. We regularly walk around our neighborhood, and when a loud dog barks from behind the fence, I give his hand an extra squeeze and say, "Don't worry; you're okay." I'm not banishing his emotion, I'm responding to it. I'm comforting him because I can see, in some sense, he has a very, very real reason to be worried.

Our Divine Parent does the same. What might it mean if every time you heard, "Do not be afraid," or "Do not worry," it was a sign that God sees your fear and worry with a desire to respond with comfort? What if this command is a response rather than a restriction? How does your relationship with God change when you read these as comforts rather than commands? How would that change the background music of your relationship with God?

COMPASSIONATE RESPONSE

It's not until well into the second book of the Bible that we see a description of God's attributes. In Exodus 34:6, the first time God is self-described, the word is *compassionate*. Scholars have found that this passage is the one about God's character most referenced throughout the Old Testament, in Psalm 86:15, Jonah 4:2, 2 Chronicles 30:9, and several other places.[25]

The English word *compassionate* comes from the same Hebrew root as the English word *womb*. When God meets Moses on Mount Sinai, the first word used to describe the Divine is a word that brings to mind a mother's care for a newborn baby. It is a Hebrew word that speaks of a deep emotion at the core of oneself. Throughout Scripture, when this word is used, it describes God 80 percent of the time, while people are described in this way the remaining 20 percent.[26]

God is moved by your suffering, whether it's physical or emotional. God is first and foremost compassionate, so you can find safety in expressing your lament, anger, grief, and doubt. You can trust that you will be met with understanding and empathy by a God who draws close like a mother.

FULL TRUTH

When we try to confine the truth of God to a set of doctrinal statements, we miss out on the full experiential truth that God invites us into. Jesus himself seemed to have an aversion to systematic theology, leaning more right-brained than logical. He certainly made some clearly worded statements, but in no other part of the Bible are there so many stories being told. Jesus gave us truth not in linear, left-brained statutes, but in right-brained, symbolic, experiential stories and images. Jesus, the Word of God, didn't give a clear outline of how God or the universe works, but instead sparked our imaginations through story.

Jesus often said, "The kingdom of heaven is like . . ."[27] I recently heard a podcast where someone suggested that perhaps Jesus didn't mean us to dissect the story for analytical data, as much as to feel the story. We could at least wonder, What if Jesus meant "the kingdom of God feels like . . ."? What does it feel like to find treasure in a field and give all that you have for it? And how does it feel, for that matter, to *be* the treasure? What does it feel like to be invited right off the street to a royal wedding banquet? What does it feel like for everyone to receive the same pay, despite the difference in effort?

Every parable is a picture, a story, something that pricks our imaginations and lands not only in our heads but also our hearts. When we sit with these stories, we find a God who not only wants to know our emotions but wants to engage emotionally with us—a back and forth.

God knows "we are feeling creatures that think" rather than "thinking creatures that feel," as neuroanatomist Dr. Jill Bolte Taylor put it.[28] Our emotions drive us in many ways and hold much more power over our behavior than our linear, systematic thoughts do. When we try to suppress our emotions to get close to God, we have to shut down a big part of who we've been created to be, as well as how we connect with and learn about God. We end up with a list of theological beliefs that don't fully engage the whole of who we are.

But letting go of our systems is scary. It's vulnerable. It requires a different kind of faith than simply affirming a set of beliefs. It means trusting that God is engaged, caring, and responsive, rather than trusting in ourselves to hold all the answers. But how do we move beyond a theoretical knowledge of God to a trusting relationship?

LECTIO DIVINA

Lectio divina is an ancient practice of reading Scripture that allows us to engage with Scripture. It leads us into a personal encounter with God, rather than trying to systematically understand the principles presented in the text. It's a way of approaching Scripture not as texts to be studied, but as the living Word. Scholars believe this type of engagement with Scripture dates back as far as Origen in the third-century church. To be clear, this is not the *only* way to read Scripture, but a way that can balance out the analytical approach that is dominant in a shutdown attachment style, helping us step into emotional engagement with God. It shifts the focus from the cold, hard facts to our own experience.

There are four movements to *lectio divina*. Many spiritual directors suggest beginning with a grounding period of silence prior to beginning these steps. One of the goals of *lectio divina* is to remove pressure from the process. For those from an evangelical background, this may feel similar to a "quiet time," but the evangelical tradition has put much focus on straining to make sure you hear something from God. *Lectio divina* has the potential to be much more restful if you allow whatever arises within you and are curious about it. There's no right or wrong. Simply notice how the Scripture impacts you. Here are the four basic movements:

Lectio Divina Exercise

1. **Read:** Read the Scripture and notice words or phrases that stand out. My wife asks our kids to notice if any parts of Scripture "sparkle" as they hear it.
2. **Meditate:** Read again, and notice what feels personal to you —ponder the passage. There's no right or wrong. Simply notice what comes up as you give your attention to the passage.
3. **Respond:** Tell God what stood out to you. You may hear a response; you may not. It is important that *lectio divina* be grounded in engagement with a *loving* God. (Hint: This means if you are hearing judgment, double-check that it's not your inner critic.)
4. **Rest:** Sit with what you received from this time, quietly accepting that God is close, as is always true.

Lectio divina is intended to be a restful and curious time of engaging with God, not unlike other types of meditation.

Rather than thinking about what this time *should* be like, we open ourselves up to whatever occurs. In this practice, we find rest and even playfulness. We not only participate with our analytical brain but make space for our whole selves to show up and engage with God, Scripture, and the feelings that well up within—even if they are small, slight, and barely noticeable.

STEPPING INTO THE STORY

Another way of stepping into a more emotionally engaged spirituality is to step into the shoes of a character in a story. It's odd that many parts of the church believe that the truth of the Bible can be known from a series of statements, when the Bible itself is more narrative than not. Jonathan Haidt wrote, "The human mind is a story processor, not a logic processor."[29] Story is the life breath of our faith tradition. Through engaging with the narrative in a personal way, we can move beyond just a left-brained theology to a whole-brained experience of God's truth.

Stepping into the Story Exercise

1. Choose a brief story from Scripture. Read it through once.
2. Identify one person in the story, as well as one specific scene. Read the story again, focusing on that person's particular experience. Notice what they might be feeling, what their goals and motivations are, what their background might be.

3. Close your eyes and imagine what it would be like to be that person: the facial expressions you would see, the feelings you would have, what things would bring you joy.
4. Notice how this way of engaging Scripture feels different from talking *about* the story.

Through stepping into the story, you move out of shutdown spirituality into emotional engagement with faith, employing the relational parts of your brain. This helps you build emotional security with the God who continually responds to people throughout the pages of Scripture.

Consider taking a step outside your comfort zone and practice these last two exercises in community as a chance to connect with others in the emotional life of faith. Not only will you have the opportunity to be curious about your own emotional experience of Scripture, you'll get to share with others what God is stirring within you and hear the experiences of others. It's a way of building an emotionally engaged faith community, which creates a refuge.

FROM SHUTDOWN TO ENGAGED

You may remember Terrell and Marie, the couple I mentioned in chapter 4. Terrell wanted to emotionally engage with his wife but felt like he didn't know how. So we slowed down the conversation.

My voice became even softer as I asked, "So you're in this place where you realize that your wife wants to know what you're feeling, and you think, *That's not something I can do.* What's it like to be in that place? To feel like you're going to fail her?" That was a feeling he could talk about.

"I feel frustrated and kind of hopeless," he said. "And then I get mad at her for putting me in that position in the first place"—he couldn't bring himself to lift his eyes from the floor yet as he continued—"and that doesn't help anything."

"Yes," I affirmed him, "you get mad at her for asking you to do something you feel like you can't do. But underneath that, you're feeling hopeless, so sad that you'll keep letting her down. Like you can't get the closeness you want because you don't know what your feelings are."

Before we continued, I had to acknowledge the reason he didn't tell her about this sadness and hopelessness. "I bet you're worried that if you tell her that you feel like a failure, part of you thinks, *She'll just say, 'Yes, you are!'* That would be so unbearable because you care *so* much about what she thinks about you. So a part of you wants to tell her about this feeling, and another part is so worried that she'll confirm this feeling you already have about yourself. It's such a risk."

I paused and let this assessment sit in. He nodded slowly.

"Wow," I continued, "you've said you don't know what you're feeling, but I see that there's so much going on inside that you just told me about. Could you tell Marie about these feelings?"

"I think so," he said quietly as he slowly turned his eyes toward her. He stumbled through his description of his feelings, but that didn't matter to Marie. He was only a few words in when she grabbed his hand to reassure him.

"This is what I've been waiting to hear from you," she said

softly, "and it breaks my heart to think you feel like a failure so much of the time. I just want to feel close, like this, with you."

Through our next few sessions, Terrell found that telling others what was going on inside, even if it was his insecurity or fear or anger, brought them close. It was beautiful to see the way that together they were able to bring to life this connection between them, to connect in true relationship, the way God created them to.

When you learn that God—or others in your life—won't be scared away by your more vulnerable feelings, you can have a little more actual courage in life and begin to emotionally engage with the world. You'll have a rope to hold on to when life gets difficult, and when you have that security, you can be open with both yourself and others. When you know God and others will draw near when you feel overwhelmed by emotion, you can take the risk of opening your eyes to the suffering around you. You won't have to hold all the answers to keep uncomfortable emotions at bay, because when you can talk with others and God about them, you'll have what you need to weather emotional storms together.

Once you notice your feelings and learn to ride the wave of emotions (what's going on in the basement), you'll feel calmer—not just looking calm on the outside but actually being at home in your own body. When you are in touch with your emotions, you feel all the more connected with your Divine Parent, sharing your whole self with a God who longs to see and know you—and who longs for you to feel seen, known, and loved.

Chapter Nine

FROM SHAME TO DELIGHT

My grandmother was the biggest evangelist in my life. Growing up a pastor's kid, I heard a lot of stories about God and what it meant to follow Jesus, constantly learning about the Bible, things like the fruit of the Spirit and the armor of God. But my grandmother continually talked to me about "asking Jesus into my heart." Her life revolved around the basic gospel message. She followed Billy Graham and Luis Palau around the world on revival tours and led 5-Day Clubs, which were short programs for neighborhood kids that explained the basic good news. She would do the same with her grandkids, telling us over and over the basic tenets of the faith and the steps to salvation.

What I remember most about her evangelistic endeavors was how she would sew away, creating what seemed like hundreds of "wordless books" from boxes of wool felt stacked next to her Singer machine. A wordless book can take many forms, but the basic concept is a "book" composed of five pages, each a simple solid color. My grandmother's books were more durable than paper; they were made of five small sheets of colored felt, bound at the edge with a simple seam. The book speaks silently through the symbolism of the colors of each page rather than with explicit words, giving the evangelistic tool its name.

The first page was black, which represents our sinful hearts. "Our hearts are no longer clean"[1] because we've done things like lying to our parents, disrespecting teachers, sneaking extra candy, and "because God is perfectly clean, he can only allow those with clean hearts into heaven."[2] The black page is followed by other colors that explain how Jesus's *red* blood washes our hearts, making them as *white* as snow (this allows you into heaven, which is represented by a gold page, followed by a green page, which represents growth as a Christian).

You are washed clean *only* if you truly believe that Jesus Christ is your Lord and Savior. One evangelistic training says, "Believing is what saves—not praying a prayer."[3] I think this may have been what my grandmother was worried about, because I often told her that I'd already prayed the "sinner's prayer," but she seemed to want to double-check that I truly believed. I remember checking with myself, trying to determine whether I truly believed or whether I only told myself I had believed. It was a valid question because I didn't end up feeling like I was white as snow. I didn't exactly feel black anymore, but certainly not white. My heart felt like an ashy gray, like I couldn't quite get clean. I just knew, despite praying the prayer, that I was not fit for a perfect God who lived in a perfect home.

WORDLESS SHAME

As attachment science took hold in the field of psychology, I found myself searching for more resources. Our local library had a copy of *Becoming Attached* by Dr. Robert Karen, one of the first books on attachment that was written at a popular level (a term I use loosely because it's certainly an overwhelming amount of information and, including an appendix and index, has a five-hundred-plus page count). I skimmed the table of contents and found a chapter about halfway through the book that caught my eye: "Ugly Needs, Ugly Me."

The chapter grabbed me immediately. Up until that point, I'd read about attachment from the perspective of outside observers, using statements like, "Preoccupied people do this" or, "Dismissive people do that." But I hadn't read an account of what it felt like to experience insecure attachment. Karen reviewed a lot of academic literature but also shared some personal stories—since we all have times when we feel less secure than we would like. He showed how our unmet need for connection can wreak havoc on our sense of self. When our needs are constantly rebuffed, we end up feeling rotten for having them in the first place—*ugly needs, ugly me*. Through the literature, he found that children who had experienced extreme disconnection would often "draw themselves as physically repellent or unstrokeable creatures, like tortoises, toads, crocodiles and hedgehogs."[4] Their starvation of love created a feeling that there was something repulsive about them, a feeling like they were just as appealing to cuddle with or hold as any of these creatures.

Karen himself worked with a boy who had experienced

excruciating disconnection in his earliest relationships. He asked the boy to draw a picture, and "although his first thought was a tiger, he settled on a pigeon, which he described as a garbage-eating bird, a flying rat."[5] When our need for connection isn't met, we end up feeling like disgusting animals, scrambling around for survival, or worse, we might describe ourselves as a worm or some other wretched animal. When attachment goes wrong, it creates a sense that there is something wrong with us at our very core.

We are designed to have our needs responded to: to be held when we cry, to be hugged when we're worried, and to have our parents smile back when we're excited. Mere facial mirroring tells us that our emotions are okay and that we are loved and accepted. It's these early reflections that create a sense of who we are.

When we begin as little humans, we have no idea of who we are other than who our parents reflect back to us. If they delight in us, we learn that we are lovable. If they continually shun us, especially when we desperately need their comfort, we believe that we are not worthy of love. If we cry and no one ever comes, we begin to *sense* that something about us must be keeping them away. We begin to believe, on a gut-level, that we are revolting. It's deeper than words; it's more often a visceral feeling than a conscious thought. For many, it is a wordless feeling.

As I read about this feeling of being defective and broken, loathsome and disgusting, and unfit for relationship, I thought, "Wait a minute, I've heard this before!" My whole life I'd heard messages in church about being "ruined"[6] and "broken," the very core of me "tainted" and "polluted."[7] The black page of the wordless book spoke straight to that feeling.

It struck me that the theology I'd been given and the attachment literature I was reading seemed to be describing the exact same thing but offering different explanations. The theology taught that this awful feeling of "inner deformity" was because of things we've done—lying to our parents, disrespecting teachers, sneaking extra candy. The psychology suggested that the terrible feeling came from what had been done *to us*. The psychology suggested that we feel bad about ourselves because we've continually been met with neglect or harsh punishment. Trying to resolve the discrepancy, I did some more research.

A MISDIAGNOSIS

I knew that the wordless book—that evangelistic tool with the colors that represented theological concepts—was old school, popular during my elementary school years and fading from view as I got older. But I didn't realize how truly old school it was. Most evidence seems to show that it was first used in 1866 by Charles Spurgeon, the revivalist preacher often referred to as the "prince of preachers."

When Spurgeon first delivered the sermon titled "The Wordless Book," he presented a brief description of the symbolism of three colors. He asked his listeners to "consider our own blackness in the sight of God" and to remember that "the crimson blood of Jesus that can wash out the crimson stain of sin," which makes us "whiter than snow."[8] The day he presented the wordless book, he was speaking in the renowned Metropolitan Tabernacle in London, England.[9] But what is most interesting is not *where* the sermon was preached but to *whom* it was preached.

That particular day was not a typical day at the Metropolitan Tabernacle.[10] It was a special event in which children from orphanages all over London were brought to hear the revivalist preacher. His audience was composed of hundreds of children who presumably had significant attachment trauma, suffering from all types of disconnection from or the complete absence of caregivers. Unsurprisingly, the message resonated deeply.

It only makes sense that when Spurgeon talked about feeling all rotten inside, hundreds of traumatized children felt that it matched their exact experience. The shame of attachment trauma that psychologists have observed feels like a dirty heart, something disgusting at our core. It was a terrible misdiagnosis.

The sermon was considered a success, and a new tool of the gospel was born. It would go on to include the other colors and was used by D. L. Moody, Fanny Crosby, Amy Carmichael, and Hudson Taylor. Eventually Child Evangelism Fellowship adopted it in 1924, and it has been used throughout the world to communicate one particular summary of the gospel message to children, often by sweet old women like my grandmother.[11]

However, this tainted feeling is not a symptom of our sinfulness but of our disconnection. When we have an insecure attachment, we feel awful inside not because of our sin but because of our unmet needs. It is the feelings of distance and separation that create the intense pain of shame. It's the feeling of unlovability that feels so horrendous. Spurgeon himself knew this feeling of defectiveness: "I could not have found a farthing's worth of goodness in myself if I had been melted down."[12] To Spurgeon, this overwhelming feeling of shame bears witness to the sin inside. He found that the evidence of sinfulness was our feelings of being "filthy and worse than filthy; diseased and worse than diseased; polluted in the heart."[13] He himself had such a strong conviction that he was rotten through and through, undeserving of love.

However, Spurgeon experienced attachment trauma in his own young life. Little is known about the details, but at a "young age," he was sent to live with his grandparents. Many have speculated that he was sent away because of poverty, but his nine siblings remained at home.[14] These sorts of transitions aren't always traumatic for children, but I'm not at all surprised that he would later write, "I seemed to be all rottenness, a dunghill of corruption, nothing better, but something a great deal worse."[15] It seems likely that Spurgeon's shame came not from his sin but from being exiled from his family at a young age.

Spurgeon didn't know that those terrible feelings naturally occur in us when our need for connection goes unmet. When we don't have a secure connection, something within us begins to hurt, sometimes causing excruciating pain. Psychiatrist Curt Thompson says that when we experience this deep sense of shame, we "tell our stories in such a way that *we* are the sole responsible party for what we feel."[16] The underlying assumption is that we feel bad because we have done something wrong or not done something right. It doesn't occur to us that we might feel this way because of ways we have been hurt by a broken world.

Psychological Insight

Curt Thompson says, "[Shame] is something that initially is translated as something sensed and a child responds to primarily as a function of the body. It is not something a child first responds to by thinking rationally with words, for often his or her brain is not so well-developed to comprehend them. Rather a response will be generated largely from the neurons in the child's right hemisphere, where so much of his or her world is being lived in the first eighteen to twenty-four months of life."[17]

We live in an imperfect world with imperfect parents. Not everyone feels that they are rotten at the core, but most of us feel at least a hint of this feeling from time to time. Growing up with this nonverbal feeling that we've never had words for, it only makes sense that we resonate with the image of a dirty heart. It's a label for something we never before had words for. Shame from attachment trauma often remains in an "implicit form," which means we don't have a coherent story about why we feel so terrible about ourselves; it's just a feeling that exists deep within. So when we hear about a sinful heart, we think, "Oh, that's what that is!" and hope that God will wash away the feeling. And often we get only mixed results.

Maybe that's part of why preachers like Spurgeon have had such wild success: he spoke to a deep need within us, trying to give a concrete story for this amorphous feeling of disconnection we carry. He felt it within himself and found a spiritual framework for it that made it a little more tolerable—and that promised a solution.

But as any therapist knows, a wrong diagnosis won't lead us in the direction of healing—and instead can lead us toward further harm. So what happens when we think this shameful feeling is the cause of the disconnection rather than the result of it? As we learned in chapter 5, we try to clean ourselves up—or beat ourselves up—through transformation or punishment to try to get close to God. We think that if we can get a little bit better, a little less sinful, we will feel better about ourselves.

HOW SHAME IS HEALED

In reality, true connection heals shame. We can move toward healing only when we understand it is a painful sign that we need closeness, rather than taking it as confirmation that we need to be holier. Like an infected wound, the pain of shame tells us that we need extra care and tenderness. We need to experience a Divine Parent who delights in us and draws close because we are so very loved.

The way we build secure attachment and heal shame comes through true closeness. We need to be with those we love in a relaxed, connected way. Certain fields of developmental psychology talk about this as a "yield state." In infancy, a yield state is when a child is at rest in her mother's arms. She's not reaching, exploring, or learning; she's simply existing in the arms of her mother, a space that she fits perfectly. She looks up into her mother's eyes and sees them looking back. She feels seen, and she sees adoration in her mother's face. It creates a deep sense of lovability. That's the power of true connection. And it's the exact opposite of the process that occurs when abuse creates a deep sense of shame. Being in the care of present and responsive caregivers creates a sense of love that banishes shame.

Entering into this state of simply being with another is correlated with our quality of sleep, digestion, emotional regulation, and other important daily functions. Researchers have even found that eye-to-eye contact between mother and baby helps the baby's brain grow and develop in the ways it should.[18] Connection is core to our development, and it is this sort of connection that heals shame.

The Intersection of Psychology and Everyday Life

Just like a yield state, Sabbath is a specific time for simply being together, without any other particular goal. Similarly, immediately after God delivered Israel from Egypt—an empire that demanded more and more work—one of the first decrees instituted Sabbath, a rhythm of rest and healing.[19] Practicing Sabbath today is a way to draw close to God in a yield state.

We don't need to remain in a yield state with others all the time, but we need it regularly. We recharge through entering the safe havens that our secure relationships provide, ready to reemerge into the world to explore, work, learn, and build. Nouwen pointed to this when he wrote, "If we could just be, for a few minutes each day, fully where we are, we would indeed discover that we are not alone and that the One who is with us wants only one thing: to give us love."[20] Yield state provides us a refuge in a world of evaluation. Consider a time when you were with a good friend and the calm in your body that let you know you were safe. In a world of constant evaluation, this kind of communion restores and sustains us.

This yield state creates a sense of belovedness within us.

It's the experience of being loved for who you are (not *in spite of* who you are). It's what happens when my daughter comes home from school, my face lights up, and I give her a hug. Or when my son tells me a joke, and we laugh together about it. It's in snuggling and nearness. It has nothing to do with how we perform or being judged for how good or bad we are. Dr. Karyn Purvis, who worked with children "from hard places," found that the way out of fear and shame was playfulness. Playfulness is an activity for its own sake—there's no grand goal or function. It's about enjoyment together.[21]

Delight is one of the biggest predictors of secure attachment, and delight grows in communion, in times of simply being with one another. We need time together—looking into one another's eyes, laughing together, playing together—to feel truly connected. There's no room for judgment or evaluation in these kinds of connections.

GOD'S DELIGHT

How can we access God's delight? When I think of God's affection for me, the primary picture that comes to mind is a powerful image of love: the cross. While this is an important picture, it skews God's love and makes it feel somber and at times almost compulsory, like the duty of a self-sacrificial soldier: critically important and full of relief but rarely joyful.

Think about the joy of a healthy parent and their child. We smile at babies, imitate their coos, play peekaboo, wrestle with our toddlers, tell jokes to our older children, and play games with them. Our delight is in the gleeful communion we create together.

The promise of Zephaniah 3:17 is that God "will take great delight in you; in his love he will no longer rebuke you, but will rejoice over you with singing." Have you ever had someone rejoice over you with singing? I'm not sure what that meant in biblical times, but let me tell you that I rejoice over my kids with singing all the time. We sing all sorts of things, usually silly things. It's something I remember from my own childhood: my mom singing to us, usually songs from her younger years that we never even heard the original versions of. We knew only the line or two my mom would sing.

Yet who else do we sing to? I can't think of anyone else I sing to in the playful way families do—it's a picture of the closeness and easiness and intimacy I have with my family. I don't even worship the way that I sing over my kids with gladness. It is in times of silliness and play that judgment and evaluation fall away and we feel safe in our skin. Who cares if we're off-key? We're having fun together. This is communion. Singing and playfulness heal our shame and fear in relationships. Yet it's so hard for many of us to access this kind of connection with God.

"When theologians start talking about love," Fr. James Keenan wrote, "it often loses its visceral sense. If we take the visceral meaning out of love, we sap it of its energy."[22] It's often hard for our nervous systems to feel the visceral experience of God's delight. We need new ways to experience God. Jesus tells us stories to help spark a sense of our belovedness, although we've often missed the message. Jesus tells stories of treasure-seekers who give up everything for the treasure they've found. Growing up, I often heard this put into a pressure-filled perspective on salvation: You have to give everything up if you're going to get the treasure that is heaven.[23]

But my friend Joshua Ryan Butler says Jesus is *not only* talking about us finding God but also God finding us. "God 'sells the farm' to bring us home," he wrote. "Jesus is a treasure-hunting merchant. And we're the buried gold."[24] We're also the lost sheep that the shepherd leaves the ninety-nine for, and we rejoice as he carries us home on his shoulders. And we're the lost coin in the story about a woman who throws a party for her neighbors when she finds her coin, filled with great joy.

And of course then there's the story we've spent some time in already. In the prodigal son story, the sheer joy of the father shines through. The father and son's connection has nothing to do with the son's performance and everything to do with how much his father loves him. It's not even as though the father balances the good against the bad; he simply reaches out to his son whom he adores.

Many take the brokenness within our world and within us to be proof that God does not delight in us. John Piper has said God hates not only sin—God hates sinners. He refutes the idea that God hates sin but loves us as people, saying, "That's not accurate, it's inadequate." He states, "God hates unrepentant sinners," and, "I don't think it's too much to say God hated John Piper."[25] When so much has gone wrong in the world—and within us—it's easy to assume God is disgusted with us.

But I take the brokenness to mean just the opposite. We humans have a tendency to wreck everything in the most frustrating ways, yet God continues to want to walk alongside us, be near us, and connect with us. Our Divine Parent gently, stridently continues to draw near to us, undeterred by whatever ways we treat each other. And when we are connected, there is great rejoicing.

Friend of God is a common enough term, but I find that few people take it to heart. Lauren Winner reminds us that theologians throughout Christian history, including Irenaeus, Gregory of Nyssa, and Thomas Aquinas, have said we all—"not just biblical heroes"—are friends of God.[26] Friendship does land slightly differently than "Lord" or "King," doesn't it? Consider for a moment what it's like to be with a friend. What happens in your body? What are the tones of voice that fill the room? It may be a different kind of delight than between a parent and infant, but it still creates a connection full of delight.

TRUE CHANGE

When we experience delight, we heal. The feeling of inner deformity goes away. If shame is the feeling of being unlovable, then being loved—and knowing that Love—is the cure. New Testament scholar Susan Eastman wrote in *Paul and the Person* that she believes the apostle Paul believed that "Change happens 'between ourselves' more than within discrete individuals."[27] She argues that it is a healthy, loving relationship with God—a truly loving parent—that creates a new sense of self because you begin to view yourself as lovable. The disgusting goo feeling goes away, not because you've changed your behavior but because you've found a loving God who embraces you.

You develop feelings of shame through relationships in your life, such as parents who treat you poorly, or peers at school who bully you, or a society that tells you are that you are lesser-than based on your income, skin color, or sexual orientation. It is then through relationship with a God who delights in you that heals the shame. It's not through changing your behavior, it's through understanding yourself as beloved of God.

EVALUATION AND SHAME

We need more than just the truth of our belovedness; we need to experience it. We need to find ways to enter into a yield state with God that builds a sense of delight. We need regular routines of resting with God. Instead, our spiritual lives often look just the opposite.

Therapist Francis Broucek worked with many clients in families where the main mode of relationship was to meet a parent's strict standard. This created a sense of self that put value in the person's performance. He found that in their most important relationships, where "a connection should be, there is only the experience of being evaluated or evaluating oneself."[28] It doesn't always mean negative judgment, but that every interaction was based on how the child was performing, how they were doing, rather than the parent coming close for closeness' sake. For these clients, the relationship was all assessment, absent of true connection.

For many of us, this mirrors the spiritual tradition we've been given. Most facets of religious life have been about determining whether you're following God in the right ways. How close are you? What are you supposed to be doing next? Are you growing—or backsliding? What is God trying to teach you right now? What's your next point of growth? Church pews have a way of prompting reflection on whether you are making your way closer to the likeness of Christ.

Broucek found that this same prompting between parents and children created intense shame. It's not surprising since in the absence of connection, we begin to conclude that the disconnect is because there is something repulsive about us. The more we continue to focus on our performance and progress, the more we feel shame. When we believe shame is due to sin, then we try to get it right—or confess our way out of shame. But if we're going to heal from shame, we need relationships that go beyond evaluation.

As Broucek reflected on our need for a connection that creates a sanctuary in a world of evaluation, he thought about the importance of interactions that aren't rooted in evaluation, assessment, standards, or measuring up. Searching for a word to describe relationship that is nonevaluative, he decided simply to call this kind of connection "communion."[29]

Seems like an appropriate term. Picture it: Jesus lounging around with his friends, offering himself, simply present with his followers. Imagine his eyes meeting theirs, a soft tone of voice being shared, the presence he's bringing to them. After all, Jesus turned the world of evaluation on its head, communing with tax collectors and prostitutes and those who hadn't been washed clean in the temple system. In this state of communion, judgment evaporates, and we can finally understand that Jesus bids us to "come to me, all you who are weary and burdened, and I will give you rest."[30] This is what God continually invites us into.

Isn't this the kind of closeness you long for with God? The feel-it-in-your-body type of acceptance and ease you have with close friends or family? Imagine finding refuge with God in a connection that isn't overshadowed by judgment but undergirded by comfort.

I spent a big chunk of my life assuming that quiet time was a time to evaluate my behavior, and I've found that many others share that experience. Here is an exercise to practice a new habit of spiritual contemplation.

A Pause from Evaluation

This exercise requires a blank, loose piece of paper (not in a journal!).

1. Make a list of the behaviors or activities that you tend to think God is most concerned about in your life.
2. Next to each behavior or issue, write two basic 1–5 scales that look like this:

    1–2–3–4–5   1–2–3–4–5

3. One scale is for you, and one is for God. Don't fill out either of them.
4. Next, fold up the paper into thirds—like a letter. Place it somewhere you can't see it, such as in an envelope or a drawer. You won't be filling it out. This step is to intentionally pause evaluation of yourself while you spend time with God. Putting evaluation aside is a way to remember that God cares about more than just correcting your behavior.
5. Take three deep breaths and close your eyes for a moment. When you open them, notice three things that you can see and five things you are grateful for.
6. Your mind might want to return to evaluation, but remind yourself that the evaluation is still on the paper and you can return to it later. For now you are being grateful for what God has placed in your life.

7. Afterward, notice how your body feels. Consider what you want to do with the evaluation paper. You might want to return to it, you might want to shred it—either is okay. There will be times of evaluation and reflection on behavior, but it's important to know that you can always take a break from evaluation as well.

A GOSPEL OF EVALUATION

Shame comes from evaluation, being judged for our goodness or badness. In the Christian faith, we know that Jesus has stood in our place. We have been evaluated, and based on Jesus's work on the cross, we have been accepted. We've been considered good enough. But it doesn't always make the shame go away. There's a reason for that. Positive evaluation isn't the same thing as connection. Being admired is not the same as being adored. Being praised for our achievements is not the same feeling as being liked.

> *The righteousness of God therefore has less to do with pronouncing a dispassionate legal status than deliverance from the dominion of sin and restored relationship with God.*[31]
> —Kent Brower

We don't want to be told we're considered perfect because of Christ's work; we want to be wrapped up in a huge hug. We don't want to be acquitted of our crimes in a Divine courtroom; we want to be invited back into the family. We don't want to escape punishment, so much as we want communion. This desire makes me think of Lenny (from chapter 5), who wouldn't even mind the punishment if there was some real connection in it for him. The gospel we've been given is a stamp of approval, a positive assessment. But we don't want evaluation; we want embrace. When we think of relationship as only possible when we are "good enough," we misunderstand love.

This is the clear picture we see in the prodigal son story. The father loves his son, and there is no judgment at all as he embraces his son. He doesn't ask him to put on a cleaner shirt and doesn't seem to address his behavior at all. He wraps him in a hug. And this is where shame is healed. We will never shake that terrible feeling of rottenness through behaving better, getting our vices on lockdown, or even confessing everything we've done. It comes through knowing, on a visceral level, that we are valuable and loved, that we are delighted in for who we are.

A DISPASSIONATE GOD?

The early church fathers held a different view of God's evaluation. They would often state that God was dispassionate. While it sounds like a God who couldn't care less, they meant that God's feelings toward us were consistent and unchanging. "God is good, dispassionate, and immutable,"[32] wrote Saint Anthony. He believed there is nothing we can do or not do to change God's good feelings toward us. We experience feelings of distance caused by "the demons who torture us,"[33] that is, the parts of us that need healing, but God is ever-present and never changes in feelings or closeness.

Saint Anthony and other church fathers believed that God was never disgusted with us—a worry we can put solidly out of mind. This is the kind of unwavering delight we would expect from a Parent so perfect as God. It's like the sun. We can certainly hide from its warm rays, but we can't change the sun. We might experience the sun in a variety of ways, but the sun never stops sending warmth our way. God continually delights in us every day, all the time. We don't need to fear evaluation or fall into shame when we come to a God who always approaches us with goodness and delight. But being able to see the light takes practice, especially if we've spent much of our life in the shadows of versions of a God who does not delight in us.

SILENT RETREAT

After graduating with my master's degree in counseling, my wife and I served in a Christian organization in inner city Minneapolis for three years. During that time we tried our best to create regular rhythms of silence and contemplation. At one point during those three years, we drove about an hour out of town to a Catholic retreat center called Pacem In Terris, which means *peace on earth*. It was still winter, so they provided us with canes to walk with to avoid slipping on the ice, as well as bowls of fruit and cheese and bread.

My wife and I went to separate cottages for twenty-four hours of silence. I worried that I wouldn't be able to handle the solitude. In the past, I would've spent the whole day reading or trying to hear

God or praying. But the nun who oriented us suggested something different. She suggested that we do very little and simply relax. We needn't ferociously read or have any particular goal for the experience. If we needed to sleep, that's okay—that's a sign of exhaustion, she said. After wandering around the grounds, staring out the window, and reading a couple of psalms, I fell asleep at four o'clock, and after waking up four hours later, I decided to keep sleeping. I spent most of my waking time the next day eating the food, staring out the window into the woods, or meandering around the snow-laden trails on the property. The one thing that I took away from the time was that God loves me.

At the time, it felt like the least spiritual approach I could've taken. It wasn't until years later that I would read Nouwen's words about time with God: "The real 'work' of prayer is to become silent and listen to the voice that says good things about me. To gently push aside and silence the many voices that question my goodness and to trust that I will hear the voice of blessing."[34] Of course, it doesn't always come so easily, especially in the middle of the stresses of life. But you can practice continually stepping out of shame and into delight.

Walking in the Cool of the Evening Exercise

We can discover delight best when we set aside evaluation—even if only for a time.

1. Decide on a calm, quiet activity. Take a walk with God, or stare out the window. Putter around the garden. Put on your favorite record and do nothing else.

2. Invite God to join you in your activity.

3. As in previous exercises, acknowledge that there's no need to force yourself to feel any certain way or to have a "take away" from this encounter with your Divine Parent.

4. Afterward, reflect on how this felt compared with other spiritual activities. Were there parts that were more or less helpful? Uncomfortable or boring? What does your body tell you about this experience?

MY SECRET SPIRITUAL PRACTICE

I have an odd spiritual practice of delight that seems almost counterintuitive. I play video games as my spiritual practice. Let me explain.

I have a tendency to work hard for a feeling of acceptance. During any given hour of the day, I'm usually doing something productive. I feel most comfortable when I'm doing something that matters, so it's a step of faith to pause and do an activity that doesn't seem to matter much.

So there have been times in my life when playing a video game for an hour—maybe two—is a spiritual discipline. I waste my time, trusting that it does not change God's feelings toward me at all. When I consciously rest in his delight as I play, I find a new way of being with God that has nothing to do with how good or bad I'm doing.

Do you have something similar? Something that truly feels like a Sabbath? Do you have a pastime when there's no goal other than to be or to have fun or to enjoy your community?

LISTENING TO THE PAIN

We need to listen to the pain that comes from shame. It's such an uncomfortable experience that we avoid it at all costs. We ignore the pain, pushing it down, or try to fix it through telling ourselves positive affirmations. But really this is a hurt part of us that needs attention and care. Noticing the lies that shame tells us helps us understand what we need to hear from God. Shame might tell you, "You're so flawed that you're unlovable" or, "Since God really knows you, God can't stand you." When we take time to focus on these messages, at least for a short amount of time, they tell us about the pain we're holding and how God wants to respond.

When you feel so flawed that you're unlovable, that feeling tells you that you need to know you are loved with your flaws, that you are both known and loved. You can ask God directly to comfort you and reassure you. That might mean finding a concrete memorial of God's love, or it might mean reaching out to others. It might mean simply voicing the shame aloud to God and asking—as the biblical writers did—that God show up.

Sarah, the woman whose mother verbally abused her, whom I mentioned in chapter 5, had felt intense shame her whole life, and most of the time she tried to distract herself from the feeling, which was the best strategy she had. Over time she was able to put words to the feeling of that terrible sense of dread in her stomach and say, "Right now I feel totally unlovable." We then connected that feeling to her early experiences with her abusive mother—and disconnected it from who she is as a person. She was able to reassure herself, *I feel this way because I was told that I was unlovable, not because I am.*

But challenging the negative thoughts wasn't enough. She

needed to heal her attachment system, which operates on a level below words, by using body language and images.[35] So when she felt like a failure or unlikable, she would imagine the face of her paternal grandmother, who had since passed but was a bright light in her difficult childhood. Her grandmother was a warm woman whose laugh could fill a room. She knew that if she had any picture of God's loving kindness and delight, it was in the hearty laugh of her grandmother, so she would bring that experience to mind. She would also talk to her grandmother—in her mind—about these feelings of being unlovable and found that her grandmother always responded in a deeply compassionate way that helped melt away the shame.[36]

Shame Art Exercise

Since shame can be so right-brain dominant, I want to invite you again to explore your emotional world through art.

1. Bring to mind a time when you felt shame—whether it was an overwhelming, panic-inducing storm or a passing yet stinging pang of shame.
2. Draw a picture of the feeling. It doesn't have to be skilled. It could be a distinct picture or an abstract image.
3. Now draw a picture of the pain in whatever way makes sense to you.
4. Stop and take a breath. Notice what the pain and shame are saying. Perhaps it's a vague feeling of being unlovable; maybe it's a rushing feeling of all the mistakes you've made.
5. Ask yourself, "What is this pain telling me? What does it need to feel comforted? Who could provide God's comfort to me?

Is it God? Is it someone who has shown me God's love in my life? What do they have to say about this pain?"

When we sit with our pain, we can find what we need for healing. Perhaps you can't believe you are lovable or that what you've done before doesn't reflect on your value. Take a moment to tell God about this part, both what you need to hear and that you need help believing it.

THE FRUIT OF BEING DELIGHTED IN

When you experience God's delight in you, you find a new way of viewing yourself. You can feel safe and calm in a tumultuous world. Knowing that you are liked, loved, and accepted helps your brain shift out of anxiety into the peace that comes with true closeness. Your brain and body experience the abundant life promised.

When you feel this kind of connection, you can shift out of fight-or-flight survival mode and bring the thinking part of your brain (prefrontal lobe) online. This allows you to engage empathy and make wiser choices. Feeling safe enables you to walk in the self-sacrificial way of Jesus.

When you experience God's delight, no longer can you close your eyes to the Divine delights in others. You can see a Divine Parent who lavishes love over creation and whose heart breaks to see suffering of beloved children. As Brennan Manning wrote, "If I am not in touch with my own belovedness, then I cannot touch the sacredness of others."[37]

When we realize our need to feel deeply loved, we will cease endless striving to be good enough to feel better about ourselves. As we move out of feeling defective and disgusting to God, we enter into a new way of connection that is life-giving for us and for our world. We find that it opens our eyes not only to our own belovedness but to God's love for all.

COMMUNION

As we see in the prodigal son story, delight is deeper than evaluation. Regrettably, in many traditions, we've undercut God's delight. We've treated our sinfulness as the most true thing about us as humans, rather than our identity as created and loved by God. We've lost the picture of a Divine Parent who wants to wrap us in a hug and replaced it with a parent who loves us dearly but wants to continually coach or lecture us about how we could be doing better.

Because of our tradition, it can be hard to read Scripture and see God's delight. While so much of the Gospels is filled with Jesus's teaching and miracles, when we pay attention, it's clear that he spends a lot of time simply hanging out with people. In fact, this is one of the things the religious leaders faulted him for—spending time with the "wrong people." Imagine sitting at the table with Jesus, meeting his eyes, lounging around, seeing the curve of his smile. What would it be like to feel the delight of God on a human face? This is what God continually invites us into, ready and waiting for us anytime we take up the invitation.

Chapter Ten

THE RISK OF TRUST

"I can't look into the loving eyes of Jesus because they aren't there."

This wasn't a client, it was me. I was trying to engage in some spiritual practices to increase my own security with God, but I kept hitting a wall. I was being invited to sit with the God of divine love, but I couldn't seem to find that love. Whenever I tried to picture Jesus, he was concerned, and his concern was tinged with disappointment and frustration. I was trying to let go of the toxic theology I had ingested over decades to freely approach a God who loves me, but it felt like the more I tried to believe that God truly delights in me, the harder it was to believe it. Like Mr. Rogers, I get hung up on the judgment passages, such as the parable of the sheep and the goats, the little parts that seem to be conditions that would mean I'm out, that I can't pay attention to anything else. This is an ongoing struggle for me.

Attachment science has been invaluable to me. It has validated the reasons I feel compelled to try to perform to keep God close, the ways that I try to avoid my own emotional experience, and the reasons that I've felt so bad about myself most of my life, especially when it comes to trying to get close to God. It gives me a framework for why I approach God the way I do.

It shows me my need for closeness and helps me identify my longing for a relationship that is deeper than evaluation and more stable than my behavior. But attachment science itself does not provide any of those things I long for.

Understanding the model is the road to healing, not the healing itself. The left, logical parts of our brains begin to understand, but it's hard for the right, experiential parts of our brains to catch up. If healing was a matter of reading a book and storing the information, my job as a therapist would be much easier. My own journey of healing would be much easier. But that's not the way our brains work.

What does it mean to begin healing your relationship with God? What might it mean to trust God again—or at least to take a small step toward trusting again? How do you begin to mend your relationship with God when it's been harmed by certain types of theology that have robbed you of the security you were created for?

Attachment science pointed me down the road of searching for better news. It led me to find theology about a God who likes me. I read a lot of Nouwen and learned from other queer theologians and from those who had walked in faith with the most shamed in society. I explored theology on hell, purity, approaching God, conditionality, and how God views us. I found a much better God than I'd ever been told about. But I still couldn't trust. I still couldn't find the loving eyes of Jesus.

ATTACHMENT INJURY

An attachment injury is what happens when a relationship has been broken to a point that trust feels impossible. It's when you want to trust yet something within says, *I can never trust again!* When a relationship has been an intense source of pain, we begin walling off our hearts to survive, sometimes without any conscious intention to do so. You opened your heart to someone, and you were hurt so badly that you can't seem to open up your heart to that kind of vulnerability again. The concept of an *attachment injury* was stumbled upon, nearly accidently, by Dr. Sue Johnson and her colleagues, who developed emotionally focused therapy for couples. They found that certain couples were trying, with a good faith effort, to heal the relationship, but healing wasn't happening.

Sometimes we find ourselves in this same place with God. We want to trust, but we've had to wall ourselves off to survive. The wall feels immovable and deeper than our conscious will to trust. It's like getting to the high-diving board, and your brain can't get your legs to make the jump. Your head knows it will be fine, but your gut tells you it's too big of a risk.

We can learn that God is dedicated to sticking it out with us, wants to meet us in our painful emotions, and delights in us the way a good parent loves their child. We can know these things and still struggle to let our bodies relax into that truth. There's something inside that says that you can't trust God. You've learned, somewhere deep in your bones, that God is not *that* good. Despite what you want to believe, you feel that if you don't constantly cling to God, you'll be abandoned. Or you've experienced over and over that your messy, foul emotions are too much for the life of faith. Or the message that God is disgusted with you has been drilled down deep. Of course it's hard to trust. Your attachment has been injured.

I've been hurt plenty of times by a distorted picture of a

God that has continually met me with judgment when I desperately needed understanding and compassion. After all the pain, I noticed that when I would reach out to connect with God, something within me winced, bracing for pain. I felt stuck, wanting closeness but also having difficulty trusting. I didn't know how to move forward.

I don't believe God hurts us, but the splinters of the distorted pictures we've been given sink into our hearts, causing infected wounds. The difference between what we're told to expect and what we experience in faith can be excruciatingly disparate. Some of us carry literal trauma from the poisonous theologies we were raised in. The mere mention of God puts us on edge. Spiritual life has become salt in the wound of an already painful human experience. It's been another experience of feeling that you're not quite enough to get the love you need. As Pádraig Ó Tuama wrote, "Faith shelters some, and it shadows others. It loosens some, and it binds others,"[1] and many of us have felt shadowed and bound by it.

Some of us have anger. We're so mad that we haven't been cared for in the ways we naturally long for our Divine Parent to nurture us. Some of us even hate this conditional God who will accept us only if we get it right. We're resentful that we have to try so hard to be accepted. As Nouwen wrote about the common feeling of never being able to keep God happy, "You diminished me and wouldn't let me be myself. I always felt I had to consider what You wanted me to be, what image or state of perfection You demanded."[2] We want so badly to be loved and to be liked just the way we are, as Mr. Rogers would say. And in the absence of such affection, we naturally become angry. The anger tells us that we long to be held and delighted in.

Some of us have had to deaden ourselves to a venomous God who intrusively watches our inmost being day in and day out, all the while scrutinizing and judging with everlasting disappointment. Living with such a critical being in your heart all the time is like death by a thousand cuts. We are burdened by the psychological dissonance of a God who loves and accepts us unconditionally on the one hand yet is constantly disappointed in us on the other. Caught between longing for closeness and wanting to hide in shame, we eventually end up ignoring God. It's better than the pain of remaining emotionally engaged.

We experience attachment injury, feeling so wounded that we don't know how to trust again. Some give up faith, while others go through the motions, hoping something might change. Others try to "go along to get along," hiding their true feelings, hoping they can fake it till they make it. But we can't seem to trust as we'd like to. Our attachment has been injured.

FORGIVENESS CONVERSATIONS

Fortunately, as Dr. Johnson and her colleagues investigated attachment injuries, they found a path forward. They found that when the hurt could be brought into the open, communicated, and met with compassion, the relationship could heal. The healing began when the person holding the pain had a sense that their partner felt the pain too. The hurt person needs to know that their partner understands what they're going through and that they feel the pain alongside them. Without this step, couples couldn't make progress. Trying to move on and "let time heal" didn't work. As much as they wanted to "put the past in the past," the hurt kept calling. Like any wound, it needed extra care. Ignoring it only made it worse. We need to share our pain if we're to truly mend what has been broken.

But as partners connected right at the point of the pain—even if it was over an affair or another deep betrayal—they found that they could begin to trust again. There was a new intimacy found within sharing the hurt, despite that the relationship was the source of the hurt. The dynamic changed as the couple came together and the hurt partner experienced empathy. Johnson and colleagues called this "a forgiveness conversation."[3] It's a conversation that helps repair the relationship.

Here are some of the typical experiences of both pain and specific needs to start this type of conversation with God in prayer, based on your attachment style:

Attachment Pain and Needs

Style	Pain	Need
Anxious	"I've often felt like I'd be abandoned if I didn't try hard enough—and that is both exhausting and scary."	"I need to know there's nothing I can do that will separate us—and that I can relax, knowing that you'll stay close even if I don't try so hard all the time."
Shutdown	"I've had to handle my emotions all by myself. It felt like you couldn't be bothered with the things that were bothering me. It felt really lonely."	"I need to know you'll hear and respond to my worry or sadness—and that it will bring you close, not drive you away."
Shame-Filled	"I've felt like you were disappointed in me or disgusted with me. It made me feel unlovable, and I carried so much shame."	"I need to know you like me as I am."

When we share our injuries with God, we open ourselves up to experiencing the care we need in ways that are specific to how we've been hurt. Understanding our attachment styles tells us the specific kind of care we need from God. When we can name the ways we've been wounded, we can take the risk of trusting that God will respond with compassion to those raw parts of us. We can seek connection right in the midst of the pain, with faith that God will meet us there. Like most healing procedures, getting to the pain will be at least uncomfortable. But being met with Divine compassion requires that we take the risk of sharing the ways we've been hurt by faith.

LITTLE STINGS

Sometimes it's tough to locate the wounds. After identifying your attachment style, you will notice the ways you seek closeness and the insecure parts of you that need care. As we learned in an earlier chapter, pain is important because it tells us what we need. So paying attention to little stings, rather than passing them by, will give you a chance to move into closer connection with a God who longs to respond with compassion.

I've always been terrified of hell. I could never quite relax with God because I always worried, as Mr. Rogers did, that in the end it'd turn out I was a goat, not a sheep. This fear has always hung over my head, causing me to white-knuckle my spiritual life. What if I didn't have *true* faith? What if, between now and my death, I made some terrible decisions or ended up renouncing my faith? As much as I wanted to feel safe in the everlasting arms, I knew that I wasn't. If anyone could go to hell, then I could go to hell, which meant I could never relax.

While the global and historical church holds a variety of views on the topic, I've found some resolve around the anxiety for me. In the Middle Ages, Christians created art pieces depicting *The Harrowing of Hell*, an image of Jesus on Good Saturday, breaking into hell and rescuing souls. The picture allows me to breathe easier, trusting that the gates of hell will not prevail. It was an idea taught in the early church and presented in paintings in the Middle Ages.

But even after doing all the research, I found that I couldn't move on so easily from decades of trepidation. Relating to God had been so wrapped up in fear of eternal abandonment that I couldn't simply move forward into a fresh season of faith. Little stings constantly pointed to the wounding that had happened.

One night I was reading *The Jesus Storybook Bible* to my son, and we came across one of the many passages that talks about God's "Never Stopping, Never Giving Up, Unbreaking, Always and Forever Love."[4] I felt a quick pang of resentment, and as I explored the feeling, I unearthed what lay beneath it: that old sting of abandonment. I'd spent my whole life fearing hell, all the while going to church singing songs about how God's love never ends, never gives up, breaks down walls, and lights up darkness. *Of course* I was resentful. So reading a sweet passage with my son about God's unending love still stings. It tells me about the way faith has harmed me and that I have a desperate need to know I won't be abandoned to my own choices, my own self-will, and my own level of ability to muster up enough faith to be saved from eternal disconnection.

So I told God about it. *Why are you always promising to love me forever and then threatening to cut me off forever?*

I felt the anger rise up, and I had a sense, a body-calming sense, that God wanted me to know that my emotions made sense but that I didn't need to worry. It wasn't an iron-clad defense of the claim in Colossians 1:20 that *all* will be reconciled to God, but it was an offering of reassurance. God didn't try to talk me out of my feelings, but instead met me with presence and reassurance.

As I shared my anger and pain, and found it met with compassion, I trusted a little more. The walls around my heart melted a little. If God understands how terribly anxiety-provoking this whole life of faith can be, then perhaps I could trust the reassurance that I didn't need to worry. It's only when we feel understood that we can begin to trust. When our emotions are brushed aside, we might have better "thoughts," but the gut feeling of true trust will remain elusive. We need more than corrected theology; we need to know that God understands and cares about our specific emotions and our particular experience.

That's what good parents do: they validate emotions and then they give reassurance. They come in close, in the most personal of ways, and they help their children feel loved and secure and calm. When parents are at their best (which, admittedly, they need not always be), they see that underneath anger lies anxiety that needs to be soothed. When we can bring our raw emotions, even our grievances and anger, trusting that we will be met with compassion, we can begin to heal our relationship with God.

GRIEVANCES

It takes faith to bring your grievances to God. It takes faith to trust that God will respond with understanding rather than retaliation. When you bring your grievances to God, you follow in the tradition of Martha from the Gospels. With emotional rawness, she is direct with Jesus about her frustration.

Martha's brother, Lazarus, becomes sick, and Jesus promises, "This sickness will not end in death,"[5] and then Jesus waits a whole two days before he leaves to meet Lazarus. By that time, Lazarus is already dead.

When Martha hears that Jesus is coming, she goes to meet him when he's still on his way, though I imagine that "accost" is a better way of describing it. She says, "If you had been here, my brother would not have died,"[6] and I can feel the resentment. She softens, following with, "But I know that even now God will give you whatever you ask."[7] Still, you can feel the hopelessness because when Jesus says, "Your brother will rise again,"[8] she tells Jesus she knows he will rise again in the resurrection, which is a way of saying, *I don't believe you.*

We know the rest of the story, that Jesus raises Lazarus from the dead, that his sickness truly did not end in death,[9] but I still cling to Martha's straightforward statement to God in human form: "*If you had been here, my brother would not have died.*"[10] As in any authentic relationship, there's room for real talk.

When we're upset with God, there's no point in trying to avoid it. If we're going to mend the wounds we have in our relationship with God, we have to speak about the ways we've been hurt. We have to voice our grievances.

Sharing the pain is a risk in itself. Taking the first step to talk with God about how we've been hurt in the life of faith can feel too difficult at times, especially if we grew up in a community where a problem in faith led only to self-doubt and self-blame: *If something's wrong, it's because there's something wrong with you*. What a risk it is to speak our pain aloud. It's downright perilous to take a chance with the most powerful being in the universe. But when we don't take the risk, we rob ourselves of the chance of experiencing God's compassion. Perhaps the way forward is taking the smallest of steps, uttering aloud the tiniest bit of what is true. Perhaps it's something like, "I've been hurt, but I'm too afraid to tell you about it right now." What a huge risk that would be for many of us.

THE GOD WHO SAYS, "OF COURSE"

God already knows about you. Your attachment style will help you understand your own needs better, needs that God already knows. God knows that you need to feel that you are worth sticking around for, that your emotions are welcome, and that you are delighted in. God also knows the ways that those needs have gone unmet and how you've coped in other ways.

The truth is, children need parents who understand them. Dr. Karen wrote that secure attachment is built when we experience that we can "be understood instead of punished, to express anger and not be rejected, to complain and be taken seriously, to be frightened and not have one's fear trivialized, to be depressed or unhappy and feel taken care of, to express a self-doubt and feel listened to and not judged."[11] You need to be nurtured. You need someone who is wiser than you to draw near when you are struggling and to give you the support you need.

I can't help but think again of Jesus looking out over Jerusalem, lamenting, "How often I have longed to gather your children together, as a hen gathers her chicks under her wings."[12]

God's mothering character comes into focus, and we hear this yearning to bring us close and to comfort us. God sees into your inmost being—what if you could trust that such a power was used to understand you instead of judge you?

Relationship Repair Letter Exercise

Take some time to write a letter to God. Put to words the pain you've experienced in your faith. Be as honest as possible.

Refrain, for the moment, from trying to resolve your feelings through saying what you *should* feel or what the *truth* is. Just write your feelings, write out the ways you've felt hurt. Use the "Beginning a Forgiveness Conversation" section if needed.

Notice what you feel in your body as you put your feelings into words. Allow some time and space for the pain. God is with us in our pain, though we need not *feel* something to know it's true.

Step into the truth of *God with us* through a time of silence, allowing the pain to find air.

Next write down your need (again, see the previous section if needed). Then finish the letter, signing your name.

Now write a letter that you imagine God would write back. Remembering that God is not defensive or dismissive, use the following prompt to begin God's letter in response to you:

Dear Child,
Of course you feel . . .

and continue what you could imagine God saying from that point, responding to your pain.

Then imagine what God would say in response to your need.

If it's helpful, close your eyes and imagine Jesus's face and what he would say in response to this pain.

Return to your letter of grievances. Imagine your compassionate Divine Parent responding to you not with defensiveness or by correcting your theology but by saying, "I understand. It makes sense that you feel that way. *Of course* you feel angry. *Of course* you feel hurt." Every emotion has a logic to it, and when we can be curious about it, we can find the need that underlies it. Ours is a God who says, "Of course." When we know that our painful human experiences will be met with softness, we can begin to melt into the arms of a God who longs to hold us like chicks underwing.

FAITH

I recently returned to an old classic series, C. S. Lewis's The Chronicles of Narnia. I read *The Last Battle*, the final book of the series and saw it through different eyes. The last time I read it, two decades ago, I did so through the lens of trying to understand the end times, comparing its narrative alongside the Left Behind series.

There's a lot to the plot, but what stood out to me was the story from the perspective of Tirian, the latest king of Narnia, who has been hearing rumors about Aslan. Not only has Aslan returned to Narnia, as he periodically does, but his character seems different. Aslan has been selling Narnians as slaves and cutting down the majestic Narnian forests to sell lumber to neighboring nations. King Tirian is faced with two different pictures of the Great Lion Aslan, The High King above all kings.[13] One image was from "all the old stories,"[14] the other from the recent rumors. The decrees of Aslan seem to confuse everyone, but they keep repeating the phrase "he's not a tame lion" to justify Aslan's unsettling inconsistencies.

What Tirian doesn't know is that this oppressive Aslan is actually an ape-manipulated donkey dressed in a lion skin. The ape is hoodwinking the nation by keeping people far enough away so that they cannot see through the disguise but claims to speak on behalf of Aslan. Everyone is confused but goes along with it because, after all, *it's the word of Aslan.*

Yet Tirian has faith to challenge what is believed about Aslan. He cannot believe that the Great Lion could be so unjust. "Would it not be better to be dead," Tirian says, "than to have this terrible fear that Aslan has come and is not like the Aslan we have believed in and longed for?"[15] He would rather die than find out that Aslan is not *actually* good. He says that finding out that Aslan is not reliably good would be "as if the sun rose one day and were a black sun."[16] His unicorn partner, Jewel, adds, "as if you drank water and it were *dry* water."[17] They have faith to disbelieve the narrative that everyone else has been sold.

It takes courage to notice that our faith is "dry water" and long for better "good news" that is the living water that Jesus has promised. In the still-face moments, it is hard to trust that God has not slipped from our grasp or been driven away by our foul emotions or been disgusted with our dirty insides. To believe, even in the still-face moments, that God is near and delights in us, that is true faith.

Consider your attachment to God; it tells you what your needs are. It takes trust to believe that God will meet those needs and to believe, as Tirian did, that the God you long for truly exists and is better than you've been told.

HOPE

Recently I was talking with my wife and her sister about how to untangle the variety of teachings we've received about God. We want to believe in a God who is more loving than we could imagine, but doubt creeps in regularly.

"What if we're wrong?" my sister-in-law asked. The skepticism is never far away. It feels like a risk to believe there's nothing we can do to drive God away, to loosen our grip a little bit. What if our emotions really do offend God? It's hard to trust that we can bring our full selves into faith. And what if we're wrong to believe that God truly delights in us, even when we're sinful?

Then my wife asked this one important question: "What do you most hope is true about God?"

And we thought for a moment.

"I hope God will provide comfort to those who have suffered most in this life," my wife said.

"I hope God will set everything right and my kids can feel safe," said my sister-in-law, whose kids are Black, growing up in a racialized society.

"I hope God will never abandon me," I said, showing my own insecurities.

What would *you* most hope to be true about God? Sit with the question for a moment. Notice how your attachment style tells you what you long to be true about God. Don't worry about hoping for the wrong thing—Old Testament writers regularly hoped that God would decimate entire groups of people, so you can feel safe sharing your hope with God. The hope that God is able to love us in the ways we need—and to be truly good news to the world—is a deep form of faith.

LOVE

Love is an overused word. We all know that God loves us, but unfortunately, love—especially God's love—has been a word that has lost its meaning. What would it mean for God to love you? What do you long for most from God? What would soothe your wounds? We need to know we matter, that our emotions matter, and that our connection is not in jeopardy. We need a love that holds us close.

Scripture promises that "perfect love drives out fear."[18] True love speaks to our attachment system, helping us feel safe. What do you need to feel safe? Dr. John Bowlby famously said, "We're only as needy as our unmet needs."[19] Our longing for closeness speaks to our need for God. We are needy people, and that's the way we're designed. With an attachment understanding of our specific needs, we can continually look to God to meet us in our vulnerability.

Understanding your attachment style shows you the specific ways you need God to come close. You'll never live in a constant state of secure attachment, but you can either protect yourself or take the risk of trusting in God's rest, engagement, and delight. You can wall yourself off, or you can live as a person who needs love and closeness from your Divine Parent. There are no guarantees, but there never is when it comes to connection, just the faith of opening your heart to a God who longs for closeness.

APPENDIX: ADDITIONAL SPIRITUAL EXERCISES

DRAWING GOD

One way to explore what distortions you've received is to draw a picture of you and God. It doesn't have to be skilled. Taking a few minutes to draw a picture of you and God together can help break through your head knowledge and into your heart experience.

1. Draw a picture of you and God—it can be in any way you would like and any setting you choose. It could be metaphorical or literal. It could also be stick figures.
2. Then consider these questions:
    - How big is God?
    - How big are you?
    - How distant are you?

- What are the postures?
- Is there a metaphor or image that you chose to represent yourself or God?
- Does anything stand out about this portrait of you and God?

In each of our hearts lives a distinct picture of who God is, and the more we understand that picture, the better we will understand why we reach for closeness in the ways we do.

JESUS, FRIEND OF SINNERS

1. Take a moment to think about the sin in your life. Can you imagine God holding it carefully, considering it? What would God do with this sin?
2. This idea might be too difficult for some. Some of us were given such intense teachings about sin that our bodies react with a trauma response to thinking of God seeing our sin. If the idea of God holding your sin feels too intense, perhaps imagine holding your own sin as you talk to God about it.
3. Whether you or God is holding it, what would you tell God about your sin?
4. Now pause for a moment. What is God telling you about your sin? Does God seem overwhelmed or disgusted?
5. Imagine Jesus, who was regularly condemned for eating with sinners. What does he have to say about your sin?

MEETING JESUS

From Pádraig Ó Tuama in his book *In the Shelter*, I learned about a practice that originates with Saint Ignatius.[1] Here is my version of this simple exercise:

1. Close your eyes and imagine yourself walking. You choose the place and time.
2. In the distance you see a person walking toward you. As you get closer, you realize it is Jesus. He greets you by name.
3. He says something about the weather to start the conversation.
4. Then wait with your imagination for what he says next.
5. Then you can say whatever you'd like to Jesus and wait for a response.
6. When you are ready, you can say goodbye in whatever way you would like.
7. Reflect: Notice not only what was said but what tone of voice and body language were used. What stood out to you most about Jesus?

PICTURES OF CLOSENESS WITH GOD

1. Take an old magazine (or several) and think about closeness to God as you flip through the pages; what images stand out to you? What images display an emotion you would like to feel?
2. Notice what these images tell you about how you perceive closeness with God. Now take the positive pictures and

keep them somewhere special for reference when you need them. I like to use ones that feel cozy and safe. You can pull these out when you want to be reminded of God's nearness.

3. This exercise helps engage your brain in a different way than hearing statements like "God loves you." You may know a lot of theological facts about your relationship with God, but engaging different parts of your brain and different senses can help heal your relationship with God.

ACKNOWLEDGMENTS

I could fill pages of thanks to my wife, Danielle, who has believed in me in all my endeavors, has demonstrated to me the kindness of God, and always makes me laugh. Her commitment to celebration and her attunement to me and our kids is the lifeline in our family.

I'm incredibly grateful to Adam McInturf and Forrest Johnson, who are lifelong friends as well as an endless help in finding theology and attachment resources. I'm also grateful for Mark Portrait. These three friendships have created a safe refuge in a world that can be chaotic and tumultuous.

Also, love and thanks to my sister, Kyanne Bickler, who has been an incredibly supportive sister and a wonderful friend.

I would not have been able to do the work of this book without the healing space that my pastors, Sarah Swartzendruber and Kurt Kroon, have nurtured at Cascade Church, with many others, including Harriett and John Congdon (thanks for a place to write too!) and Connie and J. D. Baker.

Many thanks to my dear friend K.J. Ramsey, who has helped me work through many aspects of this book and how to integrate therapy practice, theology, and research to join in God's work of healing in the world.

I also have to mention many great friends who have supported and encouraged me and listened to hours upon hours of talk about attachment and theology. Thank you, Zech Bard, Chris West, Matt Halbert-Howen, Kyle Hara, Kurt Kroon (again, as a pastor and friend!), Matt Hosfield, Jeffrey Olrick, Heather Patton Griffin, Mark Benedict, Nate Hanson, Zach Pollard, Kyle Isaacson, Mako Nagasawa, Joon Park, and Paul Pastor. Thank you, Amy Simmons, my friend, cohost, and partner in ridiculously fun conversations about attachment! Thank you for the energy and joy you bring!

I can't imagine where I would be today without the Strannigan family who adopted me when I was a lost missionary kid. Candyce and Lindsay, you are my best friends. Shawn and Greg, you are the best chosen parents I could ask for. Plus, you all helped me somehow write a manuscript during a pandemic.

I'm indebted to the care, passion, and vulnerability of the Portland EFT Community, especially those who journeyed with me in the months of advanced training as fellow participants, trainers, and helpers. Whether you knew it or not, in a powerful way, you taught me new things about a God who says, "Of course you feel that way." I'm also thankful to Hundley Suber, Sharon Hale, and Jennifer Szolnoki for walking with me week to week in the trenches of the healing work of couples therapy.

Lastly, I'm so grateful to my agent, Kathy Helmers, who helped take a bunch of ideas and create something readable, and Andy Rogers and Kim Tanner, my editors who took it from there and helped me polish it further. Your investment in this project has been such an honor.

NOTES

Foreword

1. Kathleen Norris, *Dakota: A Spiritual Geography* (New York: Houghton Mifflin, 1993), 157.

Introduction

1. Philip Yancey, *Reaching for the Invisible God: What Can We Expect to Find?* (Grand Rapids: Zondervan, 2009), 15.
2. Bonnie Poon Zahl and Nicholas J. S. Gibson, "God Representations, Attachment to God, and Satisfaction With Life: A Comparison of Doctrinal and Experiential Representations of God in Christian Young Adults," *International Journal for the Psychology of Religion* 22, no. 3 (2012): 216–30, https://doi.org/10.1080/10508619 .2012.670027.

Chapter 1: The Still Face of God

1. Billy Graham, "When We Truly Put Our Faith in Christ, Our Lives Are Changed," Billy Graham Evangelistic Association, September 10, 2014, https://billygraham.org/answer/when -we-truly-put-our-faith-in-christ-our-lives-are-changed/.
2. Rick Warren, *The Purpose Driven Life* (Grand Rapids: Zondervan, 2002), 126.

3. *Won't You Be My Neighbor*, directed by M. Neville (Los Angeles: Focus Features, 2021), DVD.

4. Mother Teresa, *Mother Teresa: Come Be My Light, The Private Writings of the "Saint of Calcutta,"* ed. Brian Kolodiejchuk (New York: Doubleday, 2007), 2.

5. Kolodiejchuk and Teresa, *Mother Teresa*, 2.

Chapter 2: Your Style and What It Means

1. Lehigh University, "'Good Enough' Parenting Is Good Enough, Study Finds," ScienceDaily, May 8, 2019, https://www.sciencedaily.com/releases/2019/05/190508134511.htm.

2. Lehigh University, "'Good Enough' Parenting Is Good Enough, Study Finds."

3. Luke 15:17.

4. Luke 15:19.

5. This metaphor was inspired by the *Therapist Uncensored* podcast. Sue Marriott and Ann Kelley, "Episode 60: Preoccupation in Relationships—Grow Your Security by Learning the Signs of Anxious Attachment," *Therapist Uncensored* podcast, April 16, 2018, https://www.therapist uncensored.com/tu60/.

6. Eden Parker, "15 Unforgettable Quotes on Holiness from T4G18," Unlocking the Bible, April 18, 2018, https://un lockingthebible.org/2018/04/15-unforgettable-quotes-on -holiness-from-t4g18/.

7. William Marion Hunter III, "Mental Health and the Relationship with God: An Attachment and Internal Working Model Perspective" (PhD diss., Baylor University, 2017), http://hdl.handle.net/2104/10140.

8. Kathleen Norris, *The Cloister Walk* (New York: Penguin, 1997), 90.

9. Norris, *The Cloister Walk*, 90.

10. John MacArthur, *Anxious for Nothing: God's Cure for the Cares of Your Soul* (Colorado Springs: Cook, 2012), 31.

11. Francis Chan, *Crazy Love: Overwhelmed by a Relentless God* (Colorado Springs: Cook, 2013), 44.

12. Oswald Chambers, *My Utmost for His Highest Classic Edition* (Grand Rapids: Our Daily Bread, 2011), 343.

13. John Piper, "What Made It Okay for God to Kill Women and Children in the Old Testament?," Desiring God, February 27, 2010, https://www.desiringgod.org/interviews/what-made-it -okay-for-god-to-kill-women-and-children-in-the-old-testament.

14. John Piper, "I Know God Loves Me, but Does He Like Me?," Desiring God, June 12, 2017, https://www.desiringgod.org /interviews/i-know-god-loves-me-but-does-he-like-me.

15. Piper, "I Know God Loves Me?"

16. Joseph William Harrald and Charles Haddon Spurgeon, *C. H. Spurgeon Autobiography* (United Kingdom: Banner of Truth Trust, 1962), 94.

17. Joseph William Harrald, Susannah Spurgeon, and Charles Haddon Spurgeon, *Autobiography of Charles H. Spurgeon: Compiled from His Diary, Letters, and Records* (New York: Curtis & Jennings, 1898), 93.

18. J. D. Greear, "3 Reasons God's Holiness Terrifies Us," J. D. Greear Ministries, September 7, 2015, https://jdgreear.com /3-reasons-gods-holiness-terrifies-us/.

19. Joel R. Beeke, ed. *365 Days with Calvin: A Unique Collection of 365 Readings from the Writings of John Calvin* (United Kingdom: Day One, 2008), May 14 entry.

20. Krispin Mayfield and Jeffrey Olrick, "Secure Attachment," in *Attached to the Invisible*, podcast, March 15, 2020, https://podcasts.apple.com/us/podcast/attached-to-the -invisible/id1499179675?i=1000468510471.

Chapter 3: Anxious Spirituality

1. Amir Levine and Rachel S. F. Heller, *Attached: The New Science of Adult Attachment and How It Can Help You Find—And Keep—Love* (New York: TarcherPerigree, 2012).

2. Lyle Dorsett, *A Passion for God: The Spiritual Journey of A. W. Tozer* (Chicago: Moody, 2008), 121.

3. Charles Haddon Spurgeon and E. L. Magoon, *Sermons of the Rev. C. H. Spurgeon of London* (New York: Sheldon and Company, 1873).

4. Ed Czyzewski, *Flee, Be Silent, Pray: Ancient Prayers for Anxious Christians* (Harrisonburg, VA: Herald Press, 2019).

5. Todd W. Hall et al., "Attachment to God and Implicit Spirituality: Clarifying Correspondence and Compensation Models," *Journal of Psychology and Theology* 37, no. 4 (2009): 227–44, https://doi.org/10.1177/009164710903700401.

6. Kate Loewenthal, *Religion, Culture and Mental Health* (Oxford: Cambridge University Press, 2007), 83.

7. Levine and Heller, *Attached: The New Science of Adult Attachment*, 21.

8. Dorsett, *A Passion for God*, 71.

9. Dorsett, *A Passion for God*, 160.

10. Henri J. M. Nouwen, *Intimacy* (San Francisco: HarperSan Francisco, 2016), 53.

11. Nouwen, *Intimacy*, 53.

12. Walter Brueggemann, *Theology of the Old Testament: Testimony, Dispute, Advocacy* (Minneapolis: Fortress, 1997), 185.

13. Randy Woodley, *Shalom and the Community of Creation: An Indigenous Vision* (Grand Rapids: Eerdmans, 2012), 42.

14. Mark 2:27.

Chapter 4: Shutdown Spirituality

1. Robert Savage, "Happy All the Time." #109. *Singspiration Two* (Grand Rapids: Zondervan, 1942).

2. Curt Thompson, *Anatomy of the Soul: Surprising Connections between Neuroscience and Spiritual Practices That Can Transform Your Life and Relationships* (Carol Stream, IL: Tyndale, 2010), 123.

3. Romans 8:28.

4. Jeremiah 17:9.

5. Anonymous, "The B-I-B-L-E, Yes, That's the Book for Me." #27. *Songs of Cheer for Children* (Scottdale, PA: Mennonite Publishing House, 1929).

6. Brené Brown, "Brené Brown on Empathy," RSA, December 10, 2013, YouTube video, 2:53, https://youtu.be/1Evwgu369Jw/.

7. Philip R. Shaver, *Handbook of Attachment, Second Edition: Theory, Research, and Clinical Applications* (New York: Guilford, 2008), 519

8. Matt Chandler and Jen Wilkin, *Women of the Word: How to Study the Bible with Both Our Hearts and Our Minds* (Wheaton: Crossway, 2014), 34.

9. Romans 8:28.

10. Psalm 139:24.

11. Psalm 139:10.

12. John 20:19, 21.

Chapter 5: Shame-Filled Spirituality

1. Fraser Watts and Geoff Dumbreck, eds. *Head and Heart: Perspectives from Religion and Psychology* (West Conshohocken, PA: Templeton, 2013), 197.

2. R. C. Sproul (@RCSproul), "We are not sinners because we sin. We sin because we are sinners," Twitter, October 3, 2017, https://twitter.com/RCSproul/status/915249707974 365184?s=20.

3. Paul Holmes and Steve Farnfield, eds. *The Routledge Handbook of Attachment: Theory* (United Kingdom: Taylor & Francis, 2014), 25.

4. If this particular story feels familiar, Jonice Webb's book *Running on Empty* helps readers identify the invisible experience of childhood emotional neglect, in which there is no verbal or physical abuse, but emotional care is not provided.

5. Patricia A. DeYoung, *Understanding and Treating Chronic Shame: A Relational/Neurobiological Approach* (New York: Routledge, 2015), 62.

6. Robert Karen, *Becoming Attached: First Relationships and How They Shape Our Capacity to Love* (New York: Oxford University Press, 1998), 240.

7. DeYoung, *Understanding and Treating Chronic Shame*, 62.

8. Max Lucado, *Just Like Jesus* (Nashville: Thomas Nelson, 2012), 1.

9. Kristen Wetherell, "Yes, Actually, God Does Demand Perfection," The Gospel Coalition, August 26, 2019, https://www.thegospelcoalition.org/article/god-demand-perfection/.

10. Henri J. M. Nouwen, *Intimacy* (San Francisco: HarperSan Francisco, 2016), 47.

11. Nouwen, *Intimacy*, 47.

12. Paul J. Tillich, "To Whom Much Was Forgiven," in *The Inner Journey: Views from the Christian Tradition*, ed. Lorraine Kisly (Sandpoint, ID: Morning Light, 2006), 23.

13. Tillich, "To Whom Much Was Forgiven," 22.

14. Tillich, "To Whom Much Was Forgiven," 22.

15. Susan M. Johnson et al., "Correction: Soothing the Threatened Brain: Leveraging Contact Comfort with Emotionally Focused Therapy," *PLoS ONE* 9, no. 8 (2014): e105489, https://doi.org/10.1371/journal.pone.0105489.

16. Sinclair B. Ferguson and Timothy Keller, *The Whole Christ: Legalism, Antinomianism, and Gospel Assurance—Why the Marrow Controversy Still Matters* (Wheaton: Crossway, 2016), 154.

17. Bradley Jersak, *A More Christlike God: A More Beautiful Gospel* (Pasadena: Plain Truth Ministries, 2015), 43.

18. Mother Teresa, *Mother Teresa: Come Be My Light: The Private Writings of the Saint of Calcutta*, ed. Brian Kolodiejchuk (New York: Doubleday, 2007), 113.

19. John 3:30 ESV.

20. 1 Corinthians 11:1.
21. 1 John 4:8.
22. Lucado, *Just Like Jesus*, xii.
23. A term my friend Heather Patton Griffin used in our conversation in a podcast interview. Heather Patton Griffin, "Destroy the Me That Lives Inside," April 5, 2021, in *The Prophetic Imagination Station*, produced by Krispin Mayfield, podcast, https://www.propheticimagination station.com/episodes/destroy-the-me-that-lives-inside.
24. 1 Corinthians 15:52.
25. Martin Luther, *Martin Luther's 95 Theses: With the Pertinent Documents from the History of the Reformation*, ed. K. Aland (Saint Louis: Concordia, 1967), 55.
26. Danielle Shroyer, *Original Blessing: Putting Sin in Its Rightful Place* (Minneapolis: Fortress, 2016), 44.
27. Shroyer, *Original Blessing*, 44.
28. Henri J. M. Nouwen, *Life of the Beloved* (London: John Murray, 2016), 33.
29. Matt Smethurst, "Does God Love You? You Own Tangible Evidence," The Gospel Coalition, July 22, 2019, https://www .thegospelcoalition.org/article/god-love-tangible-evidence/.
30. Brené Brown, *Daring Greatly: How the Courage to Be Vulnerable Transforms the Way We Live, Love, Parent, and Lead* (United Kingdom: Penguin Books Limited, 2013), 69.
31. 1 Corinthians 4:13.
32. Mako Nagasawa, "Interpreting Jesus and Atonement—Practical Issue #6: Is Retributive Justice the Highest Form of Justice? Does Atonement Theology Impact Our Framework for Criminal Justice?," The Anástasis Center for Christian Education & Ministry, April 3, 2020, https://new humanityinstitute.wordpress.com/2015/09/09/interpreting -jesus-and-atonement-practical-issue-6-is-retributive-justice -the-highest-form-of-justice-does-atonement-theology-impact -our-framework-for-criminal-justice/.

33. James Alison, *On Being Liked* (London: Darton, Longman & Todd, 2003), 15.

34. Nouwen, *Life of the Beloved*, 33.

35. Shroyer, *Original Blessing*, 10.

36. K.J. Ramsey, *This Too Shall Last: Finding Grace When Suffering Lingers* (Grand Rapids: Zondervan, 2020), 141.

Chapter 6: A Clearer Picture

1. "Billy Graham," The Billy Graham Library, March 16, 2020, https://billygrahamlibrary.org/billy-graham/.

2. Billy Graham, *Calling Youth to Christ* (Grand Rapids: Zondervan, 1947), 46–47.

3. Jude Cassidy and Phillip R. Shaver, eds., *Handbook of Attachment, Third Edition: Theory, Research, and Clinical Applications* (New York: Guilford, 2016), 911.

4. Richard Beck, "Attachment to God, Interlude: Why Are the Churches of Christ So Fearful? Updated!," *Experimental Theology* (blog), December 13, 2006, http://experimental theology.blogspot.com/2006/12/attachment-to-god-inter lude-why-are.html.

5. Louis Hoffman et al., "Chapter 13: Diversity Issues and the God Image," *Journal of Spirituality in Mental Health* 9, no. 3–4 (2007): 261, https://doi.org/10.1300/j515v09n03_13.

6. Excerpt from Pratt's speech "Kill the Indian, and Save the Man," Capt. Richard H. Pratt on the Education of Native Americans, *Official Report of the Nineteenth Annual Conference of Charities and Correction* (1892), 46–59. Reprinted in Richard H. Pratt, "The Advantages of Mingling Indians with Whites," *Americanizing the American Indians: Writings by the "Friends of the Indian" 1880–1900* (Cambridge, MA: Harvard University Press, 1973), 260–71.

7. Of course, educating ourselves specifically about our racialized society and the way white supremacy has embedded itself in our religious traditions is an important part of

this process, but research shows that secure attachment gives white people like me the emotional resilience to do the difficult work of understanding my own complicity in racism and taking action toward restorative justice.

8. Luke 11:46.

9. Matthew 9:10–13.

10. Matthew 5:43–45.

11. John 9:1–3.

12. Luke 11:42–46.

13. Matthew 5:41; John 18:36.

14. Matthew 20:1–16.

15. Luke 24:36.

16. R. C. Sproul (@RCSproul), "A god who is all love, all grace, all mercy, no sovereignty, no justice, no holiness, and no wrath is an idol," Twitter, November 17, 2015, 6:57 a.m., https://twitter.com/RCSproul/status/666585908691496960.

Chapter 7: From Anxiety to Rest

1. John Bowlby, "Grief and Mourning in Infancy and Early Childhood," *The Psychoanalytic Study of the Child* 15, no. 1 (1960): 22, https://doi.org10.1080/00797308.1960.11822566.

2. Bowlby, "Grief and Mourning in Infancy and Early Childhood," 23.

3. Bowlby, "Grief and Mourning in Infancy and Early Childhood," 23.

4. Bowlby, "Grief and Mourning in Infancy and Early Childhood," 22.

5. Daniel J. Siegel and Tina Payne Bryson, *The Whole-Brain Child: 12 Revolutionary Strategies to Nurture Your Child's Developing Mind* (New York: Random House, 2011), 25.

6. Siegel and Bryson, *The Whole-Brain Child*, 25.

7. Siegel and Bryson, *The Whole-Brain Child*, 25.

8. Siegel and Bryson, *The Whole-Brain Child*, 27.

9. Genesis 4:1–16.

10. Genesis 27–28.
11. Exodus 2:11–3:6.
12. Acts 8:1–3; 9:1–19.
13. Matthew 23:37.
14. Romans 12:1.
15. Ephesians 5:1–2, 7–9.
16. 1 Corinthians 4:13–15 ESV.
17. Deuteronomy 10:12–13.
18. Isaiah 19:16.
19. Isaiah 19:25.
20. Peter Manns and Harding Meyer, eds., *Luther's Ecumenical Significance: An Interconfessional Consultation* (Philadelphia: Fortress, 1984), 30.
21. Manns and Meyer, *Luther's Ecumenical Significance*, 42.
22. Wilda Gafney, *Womanist Midrash: A Reintroduction to the Women of the Torah and the Throne* (Louisville: Westminster John Knox, 2017), 107.
23. Gafney, *Womanist Midrash*, 107.
24. Stephen Burnhope, *Atonement and the New Perspective: The God of Israel, Covenant, and the Cross* (Eugene, OR: Wipf & Stock, 2018), 185.
25. Mark 2:27.
26. Find their list of resources for understanding Jewish law at "The Law," BibleProject, accessed July 9, 2021, https://bibleproject.com/learn/the-law/.
27. Miroslav Volf, "The Lamb of God and the Sin of the World," in *Christianity in Jewish Terms*, ed. Tivka Frymer-Kensky et al. (New York: Basic, 2002), 313–19.
28. John H. Walton and J. Harvey Walton, *The Lost World of the Torah: Law as Covenant and Wisdom in Ancient Context* (Downers Grove, IL: IVP Academic, 2019), 54–55.
29. Walter Brueggemann, *Theology of the Old Testament: Testimony, Dispute, Advocacy* (Minneapolis: Fortress, 2012), 199.

30. Galatians 3:18.
31. Danielle Shroyer, *Original Blessing: Putting Sin in Its Rightful Place* (Minneapolis: Fortress, 2016), 183.
32. Matthew 28:20.
33. Joshua 1:5.
34. Leviticus 19:11.
35. Matthew 25:40.
36. Exodus 20:14.
37. Hebrews 13:5.
38. Joshua 4:20–5:1.

Chapter 8: From Shutdown to Engaged

1. Pádraig Ó Tuama, *In the Shelter: Finding a Home in the World* (London: John Murray, 2015), 17.
2. Mark 4:39.
3. Lea Winerman, "Talking the Pain Away," *Monitor on Psychology* 37, no. 9 (October 2006), 35, http://www.apa.org/monitor/oct06/talking.html.
4. Daniel J. Siegel and Tina Payne Bryson, *The Whole-Brain Child: 12 Revolutionary Strategies to Nurture Your Child's Developing Mind* (New York: Random House, 2011), 27.
5. Daniel J. Siegel, *Mindsight: The New Science of Personal Transformation* (New York: Random House, 2010), 57.
6. Genesis 16:13.
7. C. S. Lewis, *Letters to Malcolm, Chiefly on Prayer* (San Francisco: HarperOne, 2017), 22.
8. 1 Kings 19:1–6.
9. Jeremiah 20:7.
10. Robert Karen, *Becoming Attached: First Relationships and How They Shape Our Capacity to Love* (New York: Oxford University Press, 1998), 241–42.
11. Psalm 10:1.
12. Psalm 13:1.
13. Mark 15:34.

14. Lamentations 1:2.

15. Lamentations 1:16.

16. Soong-Chan Rah, *Prophetic Lament: A Call for Justice in Troubled Times* (Downers Grove, IL: InterVarsity Press, 2015), 22.

17. Rah, *Prophetic Lament*, 24.

18. Glenn Pemberton, *Hurting with God: Learning to Lament with the Psalms* (Abilene, TX: Abilene Christian University Press, 2012), 39.

19. Walter Brueggemann, "The Costly Loss of Lament," *Journal for the Study of the Old Testament* 11, no. 36 (1986): 57–71, https://doi.org/10.1177/030908928601103605.

20. Brueggemann, "The Costly Loss of Lament," 57–71.

21. Emilie M. Townes, "Lament and Hope: Defying This Hot Mess," *Reflections* (Fall 2019), accessed April 23, 2021, https://reflections.yale.edu/article/resistance-and-blessing -women-ministry-and-yds/lament-and-hope-defying-hot -mess.

22. Matthew 6:25.

23. Philippians 4:6.

24. John 14:1.

25. Carissa Quinn, Tim Mackie, and Jon Collins, "The Womb of God?," *BibleProject*, August 31, 2020, podcast, https:// bibleproject.com/podcast/the-womb-of-god/.

26. Quinn, Mackie, and Collins, "The Womb of God?"

27. For example, Matthew 13:24, 31, 33, 44.

28. Jill Bolte Taylor, quoted in Tom McCallum, "We Are Feeling Creatures That Think, Not Thinking Creatures That Feel," Medium, November 12, 2019, https://medium .com/@tommccallum/we-are-feeling-creatures-that-think -not-thinking-creatures-that-feel-a44ff7290135.

29. Jonathan Haidt, *The Righteous Mind: Why Good People Are Divided by Politics and Religion* (New York: Vintage, 2013), 238.

Chapter 9: From Shame to Delight

1. Alvin Gan, "How to Explain Salvation to a Child Using the Wordless Book," Let the Little Children Come, accessed June 23, 2020, https://www.letthelittlechildrencome.com /child-evangelism-resources/wordless-book-share-the-gospel.

2. Gan, "How to Explain Salvation to a Child Using the Wordless Book."

3. "Free Wordless Book Training," Child Evangelism Fellowship, January 12, 2021, https://www.cefonline.com/about/our -training/online-training/wordlessbook/.

4. Robert Karen, *Becoming Attached: First Relationships and How They Shape Our Capacity to Love* (New York: Oxford University Press, 1998), 246.

5. Karen, *Becoming Attached*, 246.

6. John Piper, "The Ultimate Essence of Evil: The Majesty of God, the Triumph of Christ, and the Glory of Human Life," Desiring God, April 23, 2021, https://www.desiringgod.org /messages/the-ultimate-essence-of-evil#full-audio.

7. Charles Haddon Spurgeon, *The Autobiography of Charles H. Spurgeon Compiled from His Diary, Letters, and Records by His Wife and His Private Secretary*, vol. 1 (Philadelphia: American Baptist Publication Society, 1892), 93.

8. Charles H. Spurgeon, *The Complete Works of C. H. Spurgeon, Volume 57: Sermons 3231–3282* (Harrington, DE: Delmarva, 2013), 9.

9. Wikipedia, s.v. "Wordless Book," last edited May 7, 2020, https://en.wikipedia.org/wiki/Wordless_Book.

10. Wikipedia, s.v. "Wordless Book."

11. Wikipedia, s.v. "Wordless Book."

12. Spurgeon, *The Autobiography of Charles H. Spurgeon*, 1:93.

13. Spurgeon, *The Autobiography of Charles H. Spurgeon*, 1:337.

14. Kathy L. McFarland, "The Raising of Charles Spurgeon in His Early Years," Becker Bible Teacher Resources, March 7, 2013, https://biblestudydata.com/moodle/mod/page/view.php?id=271.

15. Charles Haddon Spurgeon, Susannah Spurgeon, and Joseph William Harrald, *The Autobiography of Charles H. Spurgeon: 1854–1860* (Chicago: F. H. Revell, 1899), 93.

16. Curt Thompson, *The Soul of Shame: Retelling the Stories We Believe about Ourselves* (Downers Grove, IL: InterVarsity Press, 2015), 84.

17. Thompson, *The Soul of Shame*, 63.

18. Allan N. Schore, *Affect Regulation and the Origin of the Self: The Neurobiology of Emotional Development* (New York: Routledge, 2015), 76.

19. Exodus 20:8.

20. Henri J. M. Nouwen, *You Are the Beloved: Daily Meditations for Spiritual Living*, comp. and ed. Gabrielle Earnshaw (New York: Convergent, 2017), 22.

21. Dr. Karyn Purvis, "Give Your Child Playfulness," Empowered to Connect, April 3, 2019, https://empoweredtoconnect.org /give-your-child-playfulness/.

22. James F. Keenan, *Moral Wisdom: Lessons and Texts from the Catholic Tradition* (Lanham, MD: Rowman & Littlefield, 2004), 12.

23. The paradox here is that while we are called to lose our lives in order to save them—a teaching in all four gospels—God is always on the move to restore the lost. We lose ourselves, in some sense, and God finds us.

24. Joshua Ryan Butler, *The Pursuing God: A Reckless, Irrational, Obsessed Love That's Dying to Bring Us Home* (Nashville: Thomas Nelson, 2016), 82.

25. John Piper, "Those He Called He Also Justified," Desiring God, October 27, 1985, https://www.desiringgod.org /messages/those-whom-he-called-he-also-justified-part-1.

26. Lauren F. Winner, *Wearing God: Clothing, Laughter, Fire, and Other Overlooked Ways of Meeting God* (New York: HarperOne, 2015), 143.

27. Susan Grove Eastman, *Paul and the Person: Reframing Paul's Anthropology* (Grand Rapids: Eerdmans, 2017), 99.
28. Francis J. Broucek, *Shame and the Self* (New York: Guilford, 1991), 34.
29. Broucek, *Shame and the Self*, 34.
30. Matthew 11:28.
31. Kent Brower, *Living as God's Holy People: Holiness and Community in Paul* (Milton Keynes, UK: Paternoster, 2014), 9.
32. Saint Anthony, *Philokalia*, vol. 1, trans. G. E. H. Palmer, Philip Sherrard, and Bishop Kallistos Ware (London: Faber & Faber, 1986), 352.
33. Anthony, *Philokalia*, vol. 1, trans. Palmer, Sherrard, and Kallistos Ware, 352.
34. Henri J. M. Nouwen, *Life of the Beloved* (London: John Murray, 2016), 76.
35. Susan M. Johnson, *Attachment Theory in Practice: Emotionally Focused Therapy (EFT) with Individuals, Couples, and Families* (New York: Guilford, 2019).
36. This path of healing is informed largely by emotionally focused therapy for individuals, and I'm greatly indebted to Sue Johnson's work. There are many therapists throughout the US trained in this attachment-based modality, and you can search for a therapist near you at https://iceeft.com.
37. Brennan Manning, *Abba's Child: The Cry of the Heart for Intimate Belonging* (Carol Stream, IL: Tyndale, 2014), 39.

Chapter 10: The Risk of Trust

1. Pádraig Ó Tuama, *In the Shelter: Finding a Home in the World* (London: John Murray, 2015), 11.
2. Henri J. M. Nouwen, *Intimacy* (New York: HarperOne, 2016), 47.
3. Susan M. Johnson, *Attachment Theory in Practice:*

Emotionally Focused Therapy (EFT) with Individuals, Couples, and Families (New York: Guilford, 2018), 149.

4. Sally Lloyd-Jones, *Jesus Storybook Bible: Every Story Whispers His Name* (Grand Rapids: Zonderkidz, 2012), 36.

5. John 11:4.

6. John 11:21.

7. John 11:22.

8. John 11:23.

9. You can read the full story in John 11:1–44.

10. John 11:21.

11. Robert Karen, *Becoming Attached: First Relationships and How They Shape Our Capacity to Love* (New York: Oxford University Press, 1998), 245.

12. Matthew 23:37.

13. C. S. Lewis, *The Horse and His Boy*, The Chronicles of Narnia, vol. 5 (n.p.: Enrich Spot Limited, 2016), 123.

14. C. S. Lewis, *The Last Battle*, The Chronicles of Narnia, vol. 7 (n.p.: Enrich Spot Limited, 2016), 40.

15. Lewis, *The Last Battle*, 21.

16. Lewis, *The Last Battle*, 21.

17. Lewis, *The Last Battle*, 21.

18. 1 John 4:18.

19. Amir Levine and Rachel S. F. Heller, *Attached: The New Science of Adult Attachment and How It Can Help You Find—And Keep—Love* (New York: TarcherPerigree, 2012), 21.

Appendix: Additional Spiritual Exercises

1. Pádraig Ó Tuama, *In the Shelter: Finding a Home in the World* (London: John Murray, 2015), 63.

The information in this book has been carefully researched by the author and is intended to be a source of information only. While the methods contained herein can and do work, readers are urged to consult with their physicians or other professional advisors to address specific medical or other issues. The author and the publisher assume no responsibility for any injuries suffered or damages or losses incurred during or as a result of the use or application of the information contained herein.